Cartwheels
on the Keyboard

Computer-Based Literacy Instruction
in an Elementary Classroom

Maureen Carroll
Pleasanton, California, USA

INTERNATIONAL
Reading
Association

800 Barksdale Road, PO Box 8139
Newark, Delaware 19714-8139, USA
www.reading.org

The International Reading Association attempts, through its publications, to provide a forum for a wide spectrum of opinions on reading. This policy permits divergent viewpoints without implying the endorsement of the Association.

Editorial Director, Books and Special Projects   Matthew W. Baker
Managing Editor   Shannon T. Fortner
Permissions Editor   Janet S. Parrack
Acquisitions and Communications Coordinator   Corinne M. Mooney
Associate Editor, Books and Special Projects   Sara J. Murphy
Assistant Editor   Charlene M. Nichols
Administrative Assistant   Michele Jester
Senior Editorial Assistant   Tyanna L. Collins
Production Department Manager   Iona Muscella
Supervisor, Electronic Publishing   Anette Schütz
Senior Electronic Publishing Specialist   Cheryl J. Strum
Electronic Publishing Specialist   R. Lynn Harrison
Proofreader   Elizabeth C. Hunt

Project Editor   Charlene M. Nichols

Cover Design   Linda Steere

Web addresses in this book were correct as of the publication date but may have become inactive or otherwise modified since that time. If you notice a deactivated or changed Web address, please e-mail books@reading.org with the words "Website Update" in the subject line. In your message, specify the Web link, the book title, and the page number on which the link appears.

Library of Congress Cataloging-in-Publication Data
Carroll, Maureen, 1957-
     Cartwheels on the keyboard : computer-based literacy instruction in an elementary classroom / Maureen Carroll.
          p. cm.
     Includes bibliographical references and index.
     ISBN 0-87207-552-4
     1. Language arts (Elementary)—United States—Computer-assisted instruction—Case studies.   2. Computers and literacy—United States—Case studies.   3. Internet in education—United States—Case studies.   I. Title.
     LB1576.7.C36 2004
     372.6'078'5--dc22
                                                                                                2004007898

Contents

Note From the Series Editor

It is a pleasure to introduce readers to Maureen Carroll and the classroom teacher and second- and third-grade students about whom Maureen writes in *Cartwheels on the Keyboard: Computer-Based Literacy Instruction in an Elementary Classroom*.

In this book, Maureen carefully describes the literacy activities that occurred across a six-month time period in Ms. Coltrane's classroom. Throughout the book, we are provided the opportunity to look closely at how Ms. Coltrane and her students use computer technology to foster literacy learning. Key to successful learning is Ms. Coltrane's ability to design creative activities that engage students in their own learning. She also is skillful in encouraging students to interact with peers as well as critically analyze the programs and tools that they use. I am pleased to see that this important, research-based account of one teacher's work was selected by a respected panel of literacy experts to be published in the Kids InSight (KI) series; I believe that the book makes an outstanding contribution to the field of elementary-level students' literacy development.

The KI series provides practical information for K–12 teachers and brings to the fore the voices of and stories about children and adolescents as the basis for instructional decisions. Books in the series are designed to encourage educators to address the challenge of meeting the literacy needs of all students as individuals and learners in and out of our classrooms, while recognizing that there are no easy answers or quick fixes to achieve this goal. Sociocultural perspectives of how students learn are the foundation of each KI book, and authors address learners' emotional, affective, and cognitive development. Strategies and actions embraced by teachers described in KI books include the following:

- dialoguing with other professionals;
- reading research findings in literacy and education;
- inquiring into teaching and learning processes;
- observing, talking with, and listening to students;
- documenting successful practices; and
- reflecting on literacy events using writing and analysis.

Authors of these books allow us to see into classrooms or view students' lives outside school to learn about the thoughts and dreams of young people, as well as the goals and planning processes of teachers. Finally, we are privy to how events actually unfold during formal and informal lessons—the successful and the less-than-successful moments—through the use of transcripts and interview comments woven throughout KI books.

As we read *Cartwheels on the Keyboard: Computer-Based Literacy Instruction in an Elementary Classroom*, Maureen shows us how to keep students *in sight* as she describes what they do when they use computers within the literacy curriculum, including how they interact with one another, with the teacher, and with the programs or tools they are given. Maureen allows us to see what roles individual students assume when working on particular technology activities. We also see how these roles shift and change depending on how the activity is set up, the group of students involved, and the role that the teacher assumes in helping students stay focused and engaged in meaningful, important literacy work. A powerful characteristic of the teacher, Ms. Coltrane, is her focus on the affective dimensions of students' learning. She is skilled in learning about and then building curriculum activities around the popular culture interests of her students. In her classroom, it is not uncommon to hear second and third graders sharing stories with their teacher about their American Girl dolls or the music of Britney Spears. Ms. Coltrane listens carefully, respects her students' perspectives, and weaves their interests with important skills that students need to develop. A wonderful example of this is a classroom discussion about "the biggest thing in the world." Ms. Coltrane urges students to call out responses—many of which reflect their favorite computer programs, special TV shows, or reading interests. She skillfully builds on these responses to work on the concept of big, bigger, biggest. Within the lesson we see a teacher who encourages students' responses; asks questions to promote thinking, not provide answers; and helps students learn how to listen to one another and respect what can be learned from peers. She wants students to value the words they use to talk with peers and understand how people need to negotiate meaning with others. She knows this is a critical part of their work together as they use limited and shared technology resources in the classroom.

Maureen Carroll, Ms. Coltrane, and the students also help us glean insights as we examine what they do to address tensions that arise during literacy practices. For example, during the six-month period, students worked on projects that required them to use the Internet and obtain information from several different sources. Often students struggled with what ideas to use in their work. Computers provided many opportunities for students to see how an author could express him- or herself—not only in writing but with various forms of print and graphics added to or used in lieu of their words. Students could listen to stories on the computer, type in their own responses or new stories, add special objects or colors to their writing, and reflect on their own work or that of peers. Ms. Coltrane and her students found that all the second and third graders did not respond in the same way to assignments—children used different paths and methods to start work, solve problems, and complete assignments. It was useful for students to see these various processes.

In addition, I gained great insight remembering the power of games as a learning tool for literacy development. Learning is hard work, but often educators position games as lesser academic work. Students do not. Games are their way of life. In Maureen's book, I examined students' dialogue as they interacted while playing computer games such as *The Magic School Bus* and *Reading Blaster*. The goal of each game is to win, but, as Maureen shows us, the students also read, wrote, and learned a lot about the ocean environment along the way. Students had control over their learning as they drove the magic school bus from one place to another on the computer screen—many even relished getting to sit at the back of the bus if they so chose!

It was useful for me to explore my tensions surrounding what students learn using technology and games. The vignettes in the book that depict actual events from the classroom helped me reflect on my own classroom practices with technology. In addition, it was a real pleasure to be introduced to software that enhances literacy development. It was even more useful to read vignettes that show students' use of this software and how a skillful teacher helped students work with the software's embedded tasks as well as progress to innovative tasks of their own choosing.

Throughout *Cartwheels on the Keyboard: Computer-Based Literacy Instruction in an Elementary Classroom*, Maureen helps readers grapple with teaching and learning issues by urging us to write responses to questions posed, gather data from our classrooms, reflect upon what we see, and generate new possibilities for what could be. Maureen helps us understand how teachers need to help students work with others on technology tasks, negotiate ideas, and learn from one another. Many parents and educators are concerned that technology may isolate students from other learners or their teachers. They are also concerned that these activities may not afford meaningful opportunities to develop skills in discussion, reading, and writing. Maureen and the students show us that computers and technology are critical to literacy learning and that through these activities students learn new forms of social interaction that are powerful, productive, and important for literacy development and their lives.

Deborah R. Dillon
Series Editor
University of Minnesota, Twin Cities
Minneapolis, Minnesota, USA

Kids InSight Review Board

Jan Turbill
University of Wollongong
Wollongong, New South Wales,
  Australia

Angela Ward
University of Saskatchewan
Saskatoon, Saskatchewan,
  Canada

Deborah A. Wooten
University of Tennessee
Knoxville, Tennessee, USA

Josephine P. Young
Arizona State University
Tempe, Arizona, USA

Acknowledgments

I would like to thank the teacher and the students whose story is told in this book. Their vibrance and joy colored all I learned, and I am so grateful for the opportunity I had to share a part of their classroom lives. I would like to also thank all the teachers who inspired me toward excellence, who showed me how caring was the essence of good teaching, and who made me realize that anything is possible: Vincent Pirone, Mrs. Little, Brother Dave, Mr. Kabbabick, Sr. Marion Hunt, Anne Dyson, Sarah Freedman, and Bob Ruddell.

I would also like to thank my husband, who supported me in all the big and little parts of this process. I will always be grateful to my parents, who were my first teachers, and my children, who I hope to teach as well as I have been taught. I also want to thank Deborah Dillon for making the writing of this book a pleasure.

Everyday Explorations and Lifelong Learners: Introducing Computer Technology in the Classroom

Ms. Coltrane's class is learning about the ocean. She has divided the students into their respective groups for literacy center time. Five students are gathered around the computers tucked in a corner of the classroom.

Each student in the class is preparing an ocean research report. Ms. Coltrane's instructional plan is for the students to use the Internet to find information and ideas for their reports. The students are instructed to record the facts that they discover on the different websites in their reading journals.

Ms. Coltrane:	*I want you to start reading for information. Some of the reading is tough, tricky reading. That's something you find on the Internet. Work with a buddy.*
Brady:	*Serena, this is weird. I don't remember how we got there last time. How do I find it?*
Serena:	*It's right here, look. Want me to show you? I am doing mine on seagulls. Analia, look, sea otters! These would be good for you! [Analia rushes over to see what Serena has discovered.]*
Analia:	*Oh, yeah! How'd you get there? What did you do? [Serena shows her how to follow the links to the webpage on sea otters.]*
Emma:	*I got to Ocean Link. Brycen, what did you use? [Ms. Coltrane hears Emma's comment and brings over a reference book with an index of ocean-related topics.]*

> Ms. Coltrane: You can use this if you want to get some ideas for
> search words that can help.
>
> Oliver: I saw sea urchins in the ocean game we played
> yesterday. There were crabs, too, all over digging in
> the sand. The school bus took us to the deepest part
> of the ocean. We got to see all the sea life and purple
> coral. It was so cool! And I got to drive.
>
> Rhett: I wanted to drive, but you wouldn't give me a turn
> with the mouse, Oliver!

As illustrated in the vignette, literacy is a vibrant process that occurs in the midst of classrooms where children laugh, argue, question, and interrupt; where voices are raised, chairs are knocked over, and shoulders are poked by elbows. As computers are becoming as ubiquitous as chalkboards in the classroom, teachers are challenged to find ways to incorporate technology to support curricular and pedagogical goals. For more and more children, computers are becoming an accepted part of classroom life. For teachers, the introduction of computers provides a new challenge. How can we incorporate this resource in our classrooms in ways that best enhance students' learning? Sometimes decisions regarding computers in our classrooms are made without consultation or discussion with those who will use them the most. Yet, teachers and students engaged in everyday learning ultimately shape the role of technology in classroom learning.

This book tells the story of how one teacher and her students went about incorporating technology into their classroom lives and the challenges and struggles they faced. Technology has introduced intriguing new possibilities for literacy learning into the curriculum. It is visually stimulating, novel, absorbing, and rich with information resources. Students are challenged to use images, sounds, and words in new ways as they experiment with computers and gain information about how written language works. In the give and take of classroom interactions, we as teachers search for the delicate balance between guidance and freedom that shapes instruction. We make moment-to-moment decisions on when to intervene, when to step back, when to give students freedom to explore, and when to direct students' learning as they experiment with computers. When technology is introduced into the classroom, it provides us with an opportunity to reflect on many of our assumptions about teaching and learning. As we observe the nature of classroom interactions around computers, we learn more about the complex nature of the teaching–learning process. Technology may not provide us with all the answers about literacy development, but it can provide us with new insights as we see how teachers and students use it in the classroom.

In this book, I share the literacy journey of 20 elementary school students in a combined second- and third-grade class and their teacher, Ms. Coltrane, as they use computers in classroom literacy activities. As a university researcher, I was able to spend nearly six months observing a variety of literacy activities in this classroom. As I began my observations, my goal was to gain an understanding of how computer technology was used to support the students' literacy growth. My chair was placed behind students as they worked together using computers. I heard their whispers and enjoyed their laughter. And, as I shared their days, I wrote their story.

Reflection Point 1.1 _____

Examining the classroom learning environment is a valuable part of making decisions on how to best integrate technology into your classroom. A critical issue is how you feel about using technology. Use a journal to respond to this reflection point and further questions as you read this book.

1. Set some goals for what areas of technology you would like to learn about to enhance your personal growth. Think about yourself as a learner. How do you learn best? What challenges do you expect to face as you attempt to learn more about technology?

2. Learning about technology can be an important aspect of your professional development. Visit an online technology and literacy journal such as *Reading Online* at www.readingonline.org

to learn more about how teachers are using technology in the classroom. Share with a colleague an article that you found interesting. Discuss your reactions to the article. Then, set some goals for what areas of technology you would like to learn about to enhance professional growth. Record your goals in your journal.

3. Participate in technology-related discussions in different parts of your life because much of technology learning occurs in informal interactions. As you read and learn more, you may wish to start compiling a list of technology-related resources that you have found helpful. A good resource to use to begin learning about what is available on the Internet is the book *Teaching With the Internet: Lessons From the Classroom* (Leu & Leu, 1999). Or, you can use the websites in Box 1.1 to get you started.

Box 1.1
Technology-Related Websites

Beginner's Central
www.northernwebs.com/bc

National Teacher Training Institute
www.thirteen.org/edonline/ntti

Yahooligans Internet Glossary
http://yahooligans.com/docs/info/glossary1.html

Yahooligans Teachers' Guide
http://yahooligans.yahoo.com/tg

The WebQuest Page
http://webquest.sdsu.edu

Glossary of Key Terms

As I retell the literacy journey of Ms. Coltrane and her students, I use the following terms.

Computer Technology: Technology is a tool—a cultural resource—that children appropriate in the social construction of meaning. For the purposes of this book, *computer technology* is defined as an interactive, high-speed electronic media that allows the user to pursue multimedia representation such as images, sound, or textual links in a nonlinear fashion. Some of the specific kinds of technology that will be discussed in this book are microcomputers, software programs on CD-ROMs, and the World Wide Web.

Use of Varied Symbol Systems: As children engage in reading and writing, they make use of the variety of symbol systems available to them as members of a particular culture at a particular time and place. For example, children might make use of music, letters, clip art, and photographs as they use a computer to create a story.

Exploratory Elements: Exploratory elements are actions planned by children that allow them to navigate through computer programs and are enacted through purposeful manipulation of the computer mouse or keyboard.

Affective Influences: Affective influences are an important part of the developing reader's thoughts, emotions, and beliefs about the importance of literacy in their lives. Affective influences are motivation and engagement in literacy activities. This may become evident through children's animation, enjoyment, laughter, scowls, frowns, grumbling, or comments about their desire to begin to work on a computer, to continue working on a computer at the end of a specific time period, or to stop working at any given time.

Meaning-Making Process: *Meaning-making* refers to the process of children appropriating the cultural resources that are available to them in the social context. Classrooms form interpretive communities (Fish, 1980) in which meanings are continually being shaped and reformed through interaction and dialogue. This process may become evident in all the interactions that make up literacy events in classroom activities.

The Focus of the Study

I was undertaking a qualitative ethnographic research study, which meant that my goal was to gain a multilayered understanding of the perspectives of the students and the teacher as they engaged in literacy activities in the classroom (Bogdan & Biklin, 1992). The importance of listening to children's voices was the backdrop that framed my study. I began with a general area of interest—technology and literacy—but as I spent more time in the classroom, I developed four specific research questions.

First, What is the nature of the literacy curriculum in this classroom? I knew that if I wanted to learn about the role of technology in the literacy curriculum, I had to learn about the literacy curriculum itself first.

Second, How do children participate in computer-based literacy events within this literacy curriculum? For example, What did they do as they used computers? How did they interact with each other? How did they interact with the computer? What roles did they assume as they accomplished learning tasks?

Third, How do children make use of different aspects of technology within computer-based literacy events as they (a) use varied symbol systems in meaning-making, (b) use cognitive explorations in meaning-making, and (c) integrate affective elements in meaning-making? Computers provide students with access to multiple symbol systems, such as words, music, numbers, graphics, photographs, images, and video and audio input. I was interested in seeing how the students used these varied symbol systems as they pursued their goals. I felt I would learn a lot by studying these aspects of computer use. I also wanted to see how the different ways that you can navigate through computer programs and the Internet might influence students' understandings of different aspects of language. For example, students were reading hypertext links, clicking the mouse on pictures that led them to new information, and using the keyboard to control the program graphics.

Motivation is a critical factor in literacy development, and I knew that children were very excited about using computers. Because I knew that affective influences are an important part of the developing reader's thoughts, emotions, and beliefs about the importance of literacy in their lives (Mathewson, 1994; Ruddell, 1994), I was very interested in finding out how they were a part of literacy development in this classroom.

My last research question was an attempt to try to tie together all that I hoped to learn about computers and literacy: What are the interrelationships among these questions, and how does an understanding of them clarify the ways in which the use of technology can support and constrain early literacy development?

Introducing the Classroom

The Setting

Ms. Coltrane's classroom was bright and vibrant with the chaos generated by students at work. You could sense both the presence of order and the cheerful disarray that children created as they made a home there. Books were everywhere: on shelves, on desks, on tables, in corners. Bright colors adorned the walls where student art reigned. The torn edges of wire-bound notebooks, well-worn journals, and brightly colored folders resisted the order of the neatly divided storage cubbies. Cabinets, computers, and drawers were labeled, many in Spanish, and freestanding easels were used to show the daily schedule. A whiteboard hung above the students' cubbies. Four personal computers lined a wall of the classroom. A printer stood at one end of the row of computers, and a color copy machine was at the other end. Four long rectangular tables lined with bright blue plastic chairs filled the room. A cushy beanbag chair was tucked in one corner and created a private reading space. Throughout the room you could feel a warm, welcoming ambiance and the allure of a place where children are valued.

I conducted my research in this particular classroom because I had met the teacher, Ms. Coltrane, when she had taught my son the previous year. I knew she was interested in technology and was an outstanding educator. I was thrilled when she agreed to participate in my study. Ms. Coltrane and I decided that I would come into the class and explain my project to the students prior to beginning it. I knew several of the students who had been second graders when my own son had been a third grader. They greeted me by name and with smiles when I arrived. I think that this made my entry into this classroom easier. However, one day a few weeks later, I realized that the students did have some questions as to my purpose in being there. One student asked me what I was doing as I was typing. I told him that I was writing notes about what they were writing so I would remember. He smiled at me (as if in complicity) and said, "For your boss, right?" Almost always, when I came to the class to conduct observations, the students were friendly and welcoming. One time a student asked me if I had gotten down everything he said and asked if I wanted him to repeat it. As the days progressed, my presence seemed to become less intrusive and more routine.

I came to the classroom three or four times a week during literacy centers, a time of day when Ms. Coltrane used computers in reading and writing activities. I had a laptop computer and took extensive field notes. I tried to limit my interactions with the teacher and the students; however, due to the age of these students, we talked often and they freely interrupted me to ask questions as I took my notes. I also interviewed Ms. Coltrane, the students, the school principal, and the district technology coordinator at different times throughout the study.

The Students

The classroom was located in Latimer Lane School, a suburban elementary school in the East Bay Area of San Francisco, California, USA. There were approximately 825 middle class students (86% White; 7% Asian; 4% Hispanic; 1% Filipino; and 2% Other) in the school.

The Teacher

The class began each day with an activity called Opening Circle. During Opening Circle, Ms. Coltrane welcomed the students, and together they read and discussed the agenda for the day. One morning, Ms. Coltrane was wearing a long flowing skirt as she stood in front of the class explaining what they would be doing that day. Serena, a student who was sitting at the teacher's feet, was gently swishing the hem of Ms. Coltrane's skirt back and forth with her hand. Ms. Coltrane didn't even seem to notice. This simple act characterized the warmth, intimacy, and trust inherent in the relationship between the teacher and the students in this classroom and was illustrative of the comfortable interactions Ms. Coltrane invited from her students.

It was important to me to try to capture and convey in my study what made Ms. Coltrane an exemplary teacher. As I pondered this, I remembered how I felt as I left the classroom after the first week of my observations. Watching her artfully weave her way through the noise, the questions, the challenges, and the learning evoked feelings of nostalgia for my days of teaching. I remember thinking to myself, She defines the art of teaching. Because, in her every action and interaction, her undiluted laughter and delight in children's remarks, her patient explanations, her unstinting support of students' efforts, her struggles to understand and reflect on her own teaching practice, and her high expectations for students' success, Ms. Coltrane embodied the effortless grace and compassion that defines the teacher as an artist.

Ms. Coltrane was the sort of teacher who was very aware of her students' interests. Popular culture permeated the classroom, and she showed interest in what the students talked about and cared about—Pokemon, Star Wars, American Girl dolls, and so on. She asked questions involving popular culture, such as "You can't play a Game Boy without what?" in the midst of a discussion on energy. Another time she told a student that even George Lucas, the creator of the Star Wars movies, revised his work. And when one of the students' spelling words was *spears*, she said, "Like Britney Spears," referring to the singer.

Ms. Coltrane was at ease with the messiness and reality of what children say and do. When one student suggested the sentence "He belched" during a synonym lesson, instead of criticizing him for inappropriateness, she asked calmly, "Instead of, 'He burped'?"

The following e-mail message, which was written in response to my e-mail request for information about how she came to be a teacher, vividly captures the influences that affected Ms. Coltrane's career choice.

> About me...um, let's see...biggest influence was probably growing up with two educators as parents (dad—7th grade math...once an administrator who returned to the classroom...missed the kids, mom—has taught just about everything, including severely emotionally disturbed children, principal, curr. development, assistant superintendent, and now is superintendent of a school district....) Two grandparent educators and countless aunts and uncles in various educational positions. My family and extended family

are also the kind that go camping with crossword puzzles, games magazines, and Trivial Pursuit...it's serious business! Very intellectually competitive—who can come up with the best riddle, toughest logic puzzle, quirkiest new vocabulary word or bit of useless factoid info, etc. (We do this for fun! Kinda strange, now that I am an adult reflecting on all this...just the norm growing up.) Anyway, I think all this had a huge influence on my passion for learning—definite contributor to pursuing a career in education. I love the spontaneity and honesty of children, always have (babysitting since forever, swim teacher, after school program instructor, nanny)...also big factors in my choice. And, like most people in our profession, I wanted to do something with my life so that I could make a lasting, positive difference in the world. (personal communication, April 11, 2000)

Ms. Coltrane talked about her primary goal as a teacher in an interview with me.

In my experience, children who don't [have] the motivation to do something won't do it—first of all—and if they do do it because it's required, they won't continue to do it. So it doesn't give them that lifelong...um, goal, that lifelong love of it. That's what our goal is—to create lifelong learners and to give them that passion for learning. So I think that's first and foremost the most important thing. (personal communication, October 8, 1999)

Ms. Coltrane provided a model of a lifelong learner for students through her own enthusiasm and passion. She was able to create with her students a warm, caring, and supportive atmosphere, where both learners and learning were highly valued.

The Research Process

Throughout the five-month period of collecting data, I was constantly looking for answers to my research questions. I read and reread my extensive field notes, listened to and transcribed audiotaped interviews, and held ongoing collaborative discussions with colleagues and professors. In a research study, one must use a unit of analysis to study the data. I determined my unit of analysis to be the computer-based literacy event. I defined this kind of literacy event as talk and activity that involved reading and writing while students worked on a computer in the classroom. As I read through my data, I considered the mood of the interactions, the students' and the teacher's purposes, and the different roles that the students took on. This analysis gave rise to the development of my coding system. I continually refined this system so that it would provide me with the tools to be able to answer my research questions.

Then, I grouped vignettes based on the literacy events that incorporated use of the computer. These vignettes help illustrate the three key themes that emerged from the data: collaboration, exploration, and play.

The qualitative research process is complex, and many different voices and perspectives are considered in data analysis. See Appendix A, pages 116–117, for further information on data collection and data analysis.

Social Constructivism

To really understand what literacy learning looks like, it is important to have a theoretical lens that informs your research. This is governed by your views of the world and your beliefs about the teaching–learning process. I believe that the theory of social constructivism provides the best way to understand the social interactions in this study, and it enabled me to answer my research questions. Social constructivism is a theory that is based on the idea that knowledge is constructed through social interactions. As Vygotsky (1934/1978) explains, children construct knowledge using the tools that are available to them as members of a particular culture. Language is one tool that mediates social interaction. As children develop as literacy learners, they are constantly testing hypotheses about how language works. They are active and engaged in meaning-making as they talk, listen, read, write, question, and interpret the information that surrounds them in the social world of the classroom.

Students also use tools in varied ways as they actively construct knowledge within this classroom learning environment. Literacy learning in the social context of the classroom is influenced by a myriad of factors, including peer relationships (e.g., what one child says to another on the playground, who one eats lunch with, or who one feels comfortable grabbing the computer mouse from), the teacher's expectations and instructional goals, the tasks at hand, and the components of the varied tools. Literacy researchers are interested in specific aspects of the tools that are used to construct knowledge. For example, they may study the forms of print, the rhythms of language, hypertext reading patterns, or the context of word use. Literacy researchers are interested in finding out how different parts of specific tools have an impact on how children learn about literacy. In my study, I wanted to find out how computer use affected literacy development. In Ms. Coltrane's classroom, computers were tools that both the teacher and the children made use of in unique and wonderful ways. Adopting a social constructivist framework provided me with a way to view the importance of students' social interactions as they participated in computer-based literacy activities in this classroom. These ideas are further developed in chapter 2.

One way to envision this theoretical frame is to examine varied aspects of the learning environment. The teacher's goal is to create a classroom climate that supports literacy development. He or she possesses a set of beliefs about learning and uses these beliefs as the basis of instructional decisions on how to best help students. The teacher also makes decisions regarding the best ways to use different tools to enhance students' literacy development. Knowledge of the tools enhances one's ability to make decisions on how to best use them.

Reflection Point 1.2_____

It is important to pay close attention to the social interactions that occur among your students in academic and nonacademic settings. You can learn a lot about your students by the groups they form on the playground, who the leaders tend to be, and how they respond to one another in a variety of settings.

1. Choose a brief period of time when you are able to observe the informal social interactions among your students. This might be when they are standing in line to visit the library, in the morning before school starts, or during recess. Record your observations of what occurs.

2. Repeat the previous activity every other day for a one-week period. Take time to reflect on your observations. Answer the following questions:

What did I learn about my students?

In what situations was I able to learn the most about my students?

What was the most surprising thing I learned?

How did what I learned by observing social interactions inform my instructional planning and decision making?

3. Repeat steps 1 and 2 every six weeks. Compare your original observations with your new observations, and discuss any differences you may have noticed with a colleague.

The Findings

As I learned more about the students, the literacy curriculum, the teacher, and how computers were being used, I began to find answers to my research questions. I used my observations, social constructivism, and research literature to inform my findings. Three major themes emerged from my study that helped me gain insight into classroom technology and literacy: collaboration, exploration, and play. Each theme reflects how the students in this classroom made use of computers in literacy activities. The students in this study collaborated, explored, and played with computers in diverse ways that both hindered and fostered their literacy development. They negotiated power within collaborative events and struggled with how to best achieve their goals. They explored varying elements that technology provided, and they experimented and discovered much along the way. They played with technology as they had fun and learned with and from each other. Within the classroom instructional environment, students actively manipulated the mouse and the keyboard, and they experimented and learned as they made use of varied symbol systems and the rich, dynamic, and interesting mix of sounds, music, and images that the different computer programs and Internet sites provided.

What did I learn from this classroom regarding computer use and literacy? First, it provided me with an opportunity to examine how to use technology to support instructional goals. Technology's function should not be to replace the instruction that is in place, but to enhance it. The story of this classroom provides insight into effective integration of technology to support literacy instruction.

Second, this classroom provided a model of how teachers might share authority with their students as access to a multitude of information sources becomes a reality when technology is introduced. An underlying belief that knowledge may be constructed through multiple perspectives is essential to the teaching–learning process because the richest and deepest understandings come from constructing knowledge from multiple perspectives (Berghoff, 1993; Carroll, 2000).

Third, understanding the nature of literacy learning within collaborative events became critical as more and more students spent time working together at the computer, and the teacher, although setting clear instructional goals, became less visible. Through collaboration, students may gain knowledge about how to do things such as open a computer program, how to work with others, what different symbol systems mean, how to make use of varied tools in meaning construction, how to negotiate meaning, and how to participate in a classroom community while developing as a literacy learner.

Fourth, in this classroom I saw how introducing computer-based literacy instruction into the curriculum required a willingness to take risks. Technology is an interactive medium, and a user never knows the exact path that he or she will follow. By modeling an open-minded stance toward exploration, the teacher in this classroom allowed students to develop confidence as active meaning constructors. As she gave students the freedom to explore, creativity often flourished.

Fifth, I had the opportunity to share the experiences of a classroom full of children who were invited to be playful with language and computers. The children in this classroom had fun with computers as they became engaged in varied technology-based adventures. I saw the importance of affective influences, such as motivation and engagement, that are such critical parts of reading and writing development.

Last, I was able to see the importance of providing students and teachers with time to experiment, struggle, and learn what technology can do and what can be done with technology. In this age of increasing time pressures and accountability, providing time and support for learners to make both mistakes and discoveries as they use technology is vital.

Technology provides all users with the means to move across a multitude of contexts, engage in a wide variety of conversations, and experience different forms of knowledge. It is only in the particulars of different classrooms that we may increase our understandings of the diverse ways that technology can enhance or constrain literacy development. Technology and literacy are related in powerful ways. These issues are reflected in each of the following chapters as we learn more about how technology was integrated into Ms. Coltrane's classroom literacy activities.

Reflection Point 1.3

Computers introduce new ways to think about teaching and learning. Many websites provide rich interactive materials and resources for the classroom.

1. Visit one of the following websites and explore the resources provided for teachers. You may choose to browse or select lesson plans to try in your classroom.

   The Kennedy Center ArtsEdge
   http://artsedge.kennedy-center.org/teach

   Read Write Think
   www.readwritethink.org

   PBS Teacher Source
   www.pbs.org/teachersource

2. Answer the following questions about the websites you visited:

   What did you learn that surprised you?
   What did you find that can be helpful to you in your classroom?
   What did you enjoy the most about this learning experience?

3. Share what you have learned with a colleague.

Organization of the Book

In the following chapters of the book, I will provide an in-depth view of the teacher and the students and present the various ways that computers were used in literacy activities.

Chapter 2 provides examples of how social constructivism looks in the classroom as students work together on varied literacy activities.

Chapter 3 describes the classroom community and explores the norms and values that defined it. Each of these elements is discussed in relation to technology integration. The varied facets of the literacy curriculum are defined.

Chapter 4 describes students' collaborative efforts in computer-based literacy activities. Various elements of support, dissonance, frustration, and power that permeated students' relationships are discussed.

Chapter 5 focuses on how students used technology to explore different aspects of written language, sound, and graphics as they participated in literacy activities.

Chapter 6 focuses on student play and computers and how this affected literacy learning.

Chapter 7 focuses on how this study may add to the larger conversation on literacy and technology and discusses how technology is shaping the future of education.

Appendix A includes the classroom data analysis. Appendix B includes lesson plans that teachers can use to integrate computer use in their classrooms.

The relation between technology and literacy is complicated. Challenges confront us at the institutional level as we try to figure out what is best for our schools and communities and see increasing evidence of the digital divide. Computer use also affects individual students' literacy development and the teacher–learner relationship. This research study provides a small glimpse of how one teacher used computers in her literacy curriculum. I hope that the story of Ms. Coltrane and her students will provoke thought and discussion about the impact of technology in classrooms. Their vibrance and joy colored all I learned, and I am grateful for the opportunity I had to share their days.

Chapter 2

The Biggest Thing in the World Is...: The Literacy Curriculum and Social Constructivism

Lily and Elena are sitting side by side using the computer program Math Blaster *(Davidson, 1997). The game-like format involves solving math problems within the context of a space adventure.*

Elena: *I don't know how. I don't know how to do this. OK, I never played this before.*

Lily: *Either have I. You can play. [Lily puts Elena's hand on the mouse.]*

Elena: *Fifteen, fifteen, fourteens, fifteens...*

Elena: *This is the hardest one. That's the one you have to get to. [Elena gives Lily the mouse.]*

Lily: *It's a bungee jump. Come on! [Lily uses the cursor arrows to make the little space creature jump up on a block. Elena puts her hand over Lily's to press the keys.]*

Elena: *Oh, you try and get some diamonds. What do you do?*

Lily: *What do you do? [Elena and Lily move closer to the computer speakers.]*

Elena: *Go over there. [Lily hits the keyboard cursor arrows harder.] How about this one? You can't leave this one until you get to the top. You go over here.*

Elena pushes the cursor arrow and moves the space creature to the right. Lily pushes her hand off the mouse. The girls look puzzled. Lily then clicks on the Help *function, and the* Help *screen appears. They leave this screen after only a few seconds, almost too quickly to have read much at all. After a few moments, the girls realize that they are unable to move anywhere else in the program. They are lost in the program.*

Lily: *I don't get this.*

Elena: *I don't get this either.*

Lily: *Serena, do you know how to get out of this?*

Serena: *You got to do this.*

Elena: *We don't get it.*

Serena: *The number you get in your brain has to be between this and this. [Serena points to a blank space on the screen between two equations.]*

Elena: *OK, now what do we do when we have it in our heads?*

Serena: *Press* Enter.

*E*lena and Lily were not sure what to do. They engaged in dialogue and negotiated meaning together. The description of Elena and Lily's interactions around the computer is an example of what I saw in daily classroom interactions. The computer program served as a mediational tool that allowed them to achieve social goals, such as playing together, and intellectual goals, such as working to complete the math activities. In addition, the students talked to each other and asked for help when they were confused. Children's dramatic and narrative language helps them play in an imaginative world and also connects them to others. In this chapter, I examine the social construction of meaning in the classroom. It is important to see how students' social interactions affect meaning-making and what this looks like in this particular classroom in order to gain insight into the nature of literacy development.

The Social Construction of Meaning

As mentioned in chapter 1, social constructivism provides a framework for understanding the theoretical perspective described in this book. It is important that teachers understand the social constructivist perspective as they integrate technology into the literacy curriculum because this perspective allows them to look closely at the social interactions among students as they use the tools available to them as members of a particular culture. As Vygotsky (1934/1978) describes, opportunities to interact verbally with other people in the social environment become crucial to cognitive development because children's written language learning is both social and developmental.

Language is central to this view, as we communicate and engage in dialogue with others (Bakhtin, 1986). Bakhtin describes how "our thought itself—philosophical, scientific, and artistic—is born and shaped in the process of interaction and struggle with others' thought" (p. 92). How do children come to understand language? How do they use language as a tool to mediate social interaction? How do they use computers as a tool to mediate social interaction?

In a social constructivist classroom, student inquiry, exploration, and interaction are critical. In the following section, I will provide some examples of social constructivism in Ms. Coltrane's classroom.

Classroom Literacy Activities

In order to truly understand the role technology played in the literacy curriculum in Ms. Coltrane's classroom, I felt it was important to first examine the literacy curriculum itself. I spent the initial portion of my observation trying to gain an understanding of the nature of the classroom literacy activities.

A typical day began with Opening Circle, where the children gather in a circle on the rug. Ms. Coltrane used this time to welcome each child personally. The class reviewed the agenda for the day that was printed on the upper right-hand corner of the white board. After Opening Circle, Ms. Coltrane introduced literacy centers, which involved a variety of reading and writing activities. Students rotated through all the activities during a one-week period. (See Figure 1 for a sample daily agenda.)

Whole-Class Discussions. Dialogue and negotiation were central to the collective construction of meaning-making in Ms. Coltrane's class. This became evident in whole-class discussions. For example, Ms. Coltrane began literacy center time one morning by saying, "I want you to finish this sentence for me. The biggest thing in the world is…." The students began to call out their responses.

Figure 1
Sample Daily Agenda

October 14, 1999
Agenda
8:15 a.m. Opening Circle
8:30 a.m. Oceanography
9:15 a.m. Literacy Centers
10:15 a.m. Recess
10:20 a.m. Choice Math Centers
11:20 a.m. Finish Tall Tales
11:55 a.m. Read Harry Potter
12:15 p.m. Drop Everything And Read (DEAR) program
12:30 p.m. Lunch
1:10 p.m. Art
1:55 p.m. Recess
Tribes
Appreciations

The sky.

Torzon. (a Pokemon character)

Friendship.

The world.

The ocean.

The universe.

The Empire State building.

The water.

Our imagination.

When Elena said, "A tiny grain of sand," Ms. Coltrane asked her why she picked that.

Elena: Because I wanted to.

Ms. Coltrane: What made you think of that?

Elena: Opposites.

When one student suggested "the stars" Serena said, "That's not really in the world."

Ms. Coltrane quickly defended the right to suggest anything and reminded the class, "There are no wrong answers."

Ms. Coltrane then told the students to turn to someone next to them and try to define the word *biggest*. After a few minutes she said, "Think about what in your mind you think I meant by the word *biggest*."

Serena:	The biggest thing in the world is the widest. The biggest thing in the world is bigger than all the atoms. It's something that there's nothing bigger than... [She stops in confusion.]
Ms. Coltrane:	What does *bigger than* mean?
Oliver:	Greater, like math.
Elena:	What the word *biggest* would mean?
Ms. Coltrane:	What does *big* mean? This is hard.
Analia:	It's not like this. [She puts her hands very close together and then opens them wide. The class laughs.]
Ms. Coltrane:	What about what Serena said—friends and imagination? Is it a big thing?
Serena:	Imagination is your brains, and if you put all the things together it would be really big. Imagination is the only reason we are here—God made us up. Our clothes, our computers are all made up.
Ms. Coltrane:	You're saying these are all a result of imagination but it doesn't tell me what *biggest* is.
Oliver:	Like chalkboard is a little big but big is like 20 the sizes of it.

Ms. Coltrane said that she was still curious about what they meant. She told them that if they were defining words with words then they would have to tell the class what those other words meant.

Ms. Coltrane:	I'm just questioning to get you to think. There is no right answer. The more you ask questions and get our

brains going, the better thinkers we become. The biggest thing is an unanswered question.

As was evident in this classroom exchange, the socialization process consists of reciprocal interactions and joint construction of meaning by the individual and others in the social context (Shulman & Carey, 1984). When students are encouraged to say and defend what they think in discussions with others, their responses grow deeper, richer, and more complex (Almasi, 1995). As Dyson (1993) explains,

> We work to create more intimate, more particular worlds that capture some aspect of the experiences we share with other people. This human urge is fundamental to the whole of our intellectual and emotional lives, as it helps set in play the search for mutuality, for understanding and for being understood. (p. 11)

Ms. Coltrane's purpose in engaging in this exercise was to focus on the power of words in negotiating meaning. Responsiveness plays an important part in learning, and teacher and peer response to what students say helps further students' understandings of ideas. Children learn about the power of words as others respond to them. Therefore, dialogue is a central element of a social constructivist perspective of learning. As Cazden (1988) states, dialogue serves as a scaffold for student learning. Not only is dialogue important in the literacy curriculum, but it also is a critical part of classroom literacy interactions around computers. (See Box 2.1 for resources for learning about classroom dialogue.)

Box 2.1
Resources for Learning About Classroom Dialogue

Cazden, C. (1988). *Classroom discourse: The language of teaching and learning*. Portsmouth, NH: Heinemann.

Mehan, H. (1982). The structure of classroom events and their consequences for student performance. In P. Gilmore & A. Glatthorn (Eds.), *Children in and out of school: Ethnography and education*. Washington, DC: Center for Applied Linguistics.

Reflection Point 2.1

In many classrooms, teachers ask questions and students respond, yet little real dialogue occurs. This has been described by Mehan (1982) as an Initiation–Reply–Evaluation response. Instead, teachers should provide multiple opportunities for students to participate in extended classroom dialogue, allowing students to think about what has been said, respond to different viewpoints, and synthesize their own ideas.

1. What opportunities do you provide for your students to engage in dialogue that facilitates knowledge construction?

2. Collect some data that involves teacher–student dialogue in the classroom. You may use audiotapes or videotapes. Focus on the following questions:

   What kinds of questions were being asked?

   What kinds of questions were being answered?

   Who directed most of the dialogue?

   How did students respond to one another's comments?

   What did you learn from reflecting on these interactions?

Small-Group Discussions. Ms. Coltrane's students participated in small-group literacy activities as well. The following example of a small-group discussion highlights the social nature of meaning-making. We see how dialogue surrounds, affects, challenges, and shapes meaning in the students' social interactions.

Rhett and Analia are sitting side by side practicing cursive writing. Serena is working at the same table on a holiday crossword puzzle.

Rhett: I'm very not good at *g*s. I'm not good at *g*s.

Analia: I hate *w*s.

Serena: I love *w*s.

Rhett: I love *h*s.

Analia: I know, that's fun.

Rhett: Oh, look at my page.

Analia: Even though I'm good at *w*s, I hate them.

Rhett: I don't like *i*'s.

Analia: I love *i*'s.

Rhett: That one's easy. A-b-c-d-e-f-g-h-i-j...how do you do *j*s?

Serena: It's really easy. It's like this. [Serena shows Rhett how to form the letter.]

Rhett: I like *j*s.

Analia: Yeah, they're fun.

In this example, the students' intellectual work served as a means of social bonding. Once again, dialogue was a critical element in the construction of knowledge. Rhett and Analia engaged in an intellectual task—practicing cursive—and the actual work was influenced by their social interaction.

It is important to understand the various elements of the classroom curriculum and the theoretical basis of social constructivism because computer use was nested within it. With this understanding in mind, we can look more closely at computers in the literacy curriculum.

Computers and Literacy Development

Leu (2002) states that "Literacy has always been a social phenomenon, but the new literacies contain even more of a social component than traditional literacies" (p. 314). This is because of the increasing use of e-mail, chat rooms, the Internet, instant messenger programs, and new ways of thinking about the relationship between authors and readers of electronic media. Computers invite new forms of social interaction because we are able to communicate with others in new ways.

How do computers mediate social interaction? As Ms. Coltrane's students participated in computer-based literacy activities, they often tried varied strategies and asked others for assistance. They used computers as tools as they struggled to achieve social and intellectual goals. The following exchange illustrates how this occurred.

Jamal and Brycen are trying to figure out how to use a software program. Brycen clicks on the *Help* function and then quickly closes it. He uses the arrow cursors to try to move the character to begin the game, but he is unsuccessful.

Brycen: Far, oh, I know. [Unsure of how to proceed, Brycen presses the *Caps Lock* and the *Shift* key but nothing happens.]

Jamal: Wait! Let me try. [Jamal takes the mouse and clicks on the word *zap*. Nothing happens.]

Jamal: Maybe we should ask Seth. [Seth is considered somewhat of a computer expert in the classroom.]

The students' intellectual goal was to learn how to use a software program, and their social goal was to collaborate to complete the task. Their social bond was an integral part of the learning experience. Often computers are considered isolating for students, as they work alone on skill-and-drill activities. This did not occur in this classroom. As Ms. Coltrane commented, "As far as the kids interacting with the computers, I don't know, it's been interesting for me to watch too, as they're interacting 'cause they do do a lot of dialogue around the technology." She characterized her students as "really interacting and it being very fluid."

Reflection Point 2.2

How do you view social interactions around computers? Are they distracting? Are they helpful? It is often helpful to make a video-tape of your students interacting around the computer in order to gain insight into what is occurring. Choose a specific time period, such as an assigned activity, when the students are working on the computer. Initially, try to limit your observation to two students working together, and tape them for no longer than 5–7 minutes. The following directions can help guide your analysis of your students' interactions.

1. Watch the tape four times. The first time you watch the tape, try to gain a general sense of what is occurring. Do not take any notes yet.

2. The second time through the tape, take notes about different things that are occurring. Observe the interactions from one student's perspective.

3. The third time through the tape, observe the second student and think about what is occurring from his or her perspective.

4. After the fourth time through the tape, answer the following questions:

   What was the general tone of the activity?

   How did the students work together?

   Was one student more assertive than the other?

   How did students resolve any differences?

   What did the students accomplish?

   What facilitated or hindered students in accomplishing the work?

   What surprised you as you observed the students?

   What did what you learn through these observations that will help inform your instructional goals?

   How do you think that social interactions around the computer might enhance or inhibit literacy learning?

Symbol Systems, Multiple Perspectives, and Computers

Children use various symbol systems, such as drawing, music, mathematics, or language, as they come to understand how to read and write. Essentially, they are making use of multiple symbol systems in their quest to make sense of their worlds (Berghoff, 1993). Children gradually come to discover the range of functions served by written language, including its capacities for social interaction and individual reflection (Dyson, 1989). Computers give children opportunities to use a wide variety of symbol systems and encounter new possibilities for constructing knowledge. For example, children can use word-processing software that allows them to choose different graphic, textual, and musical representations of meaning. Cambourne (2001) describes how teaching–learning activities that involve learners in manipulating meanings across and within different symbol systems are more effective than those in which just one symbol system is involved. Short, Kaufman, and Kahn (2000) found that a greater availability of multiple symbolic systems gave students the opportunity to think more broadly and to consider other ideas, and it fostered connections that children could employ in gaining new understandings about literacy. Teachers can use computers to help children explore different symbol systems in literacy activities.

Understanding the nature of the social construction of meaning and the role of symbol systems in constructing meaning from multiple perspectives is vital to furthering our understanding of the relation between literacy and technology. Eisner (1978) describes how different symbol systems provide us with different perspectives on knowledge.

> Each symbol system—mathematics, the sciences, art, music, literature, poetry, and the like—allows us not only to conceptualize our ideas about reality but also to convey those ideas to others. Each symbol system sets parameters upon what we can conceive and what we can express. Thus, through painting we are able to know autumn in ways that only the visual arts make possible. Through poetry we can know autumn in ways that only poems can provide. Through botany we are able to know autumn in ways that only botanists can convey. How autumn is conceived and hence, what we know about it, depends upon the symbol system we use or choose to use. (p. 618)

Children are able to use symbol systems that they are familiar with in new and interesting ways as they experiment with computers and discover the many different ways that it is possible to express meaning. Such experimentation occurred in Ms. Coltrane's classroom as students wrote poetry using the software program called *The Amazing Writing Machine*

(Riverdeep, 2004). The program allows users to choose from a variety of options as they write. For example, students can change the font type, font size, and text style; use a large variety of symbols, including stars, leaves, hearts, trees, lollipops, pinwheels, flowers, numbers, robots, and trucks; choose from a variety of layout templates; animate graphics; and hear different types of music as they type (see Figure 2).

Elena begins to explore how to use *The Amazing Writing Machine* as she types a poem.

Elena: Oh, cool. I like these stars. [She moves the mouse back and forth in the leaf template.] How you do that? [Vanessa shows her how to change the color of the stars.]

Elena: Thank you. Dynamite! [Elena continues to explore the different symbols available in the program as she composes her poem.]

Students make use of diverse symbol systems in varied ways as they explore and experiment with different forms of written expression. As

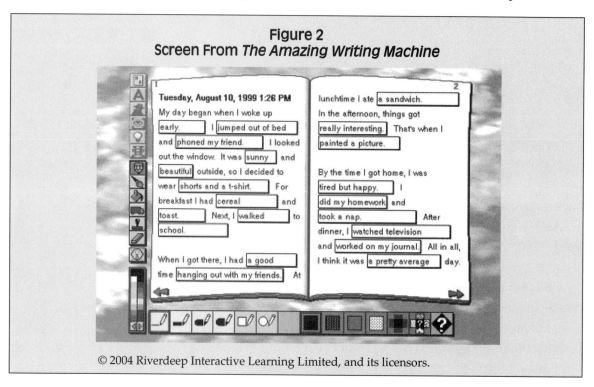

Figure 2
Screen From *The Amazing Writing Machine*

© 2004 Riverdeep Interactive Learning Limited, and its licensors.

we see from this example, Elena explored options such as stars, leaves, and colors. The ability to construct knowledge from multiple perspectives is a critical part of literacy development, and as evidenced by this example, computers can facilitate this process.

Reflection on Language and Computers

Another important part of literacy development is the ability to reflect on language. How do computers influence this process? In the classroom, reflection on language often occurs as children ponder how they are going to express an idea in writing. Dyson (1991) describes the development of the writing process as children's struggle to match their intended meanings with some kind of graphic representation. Computers provide students with easy access to many different forms of language that they can use to express their thoughts. They provide multiple opportunities to interact in a variety of different ways with words, pictures, and print and may foster reflection on language.

Students can experiment with different features on websites and in software programs as they try to express meaning in writing and reflect on the forms of language. The computer serves as a tool of social mediation as children type, erase, scribble, and fiddle with shapes, colors, letters, and graphics and talk about what they are doing with their friends. They can listen to stories, move objects and text, and add color, shades, and texture to a drawing. When we provide time for children to explore the capabilities and features of texts using technology, they gain information about how language works (Labbo, 1996). Children benefit from learning experiences that allow them to explore and experience in their own ways the symbolic and social medium they are learning (Edelsky, 1986).

As Ms. Coltrane's students explored the different options in their word-processing software, they had the opportunity to view varied ways to express and capture meaning. Different children use different forms of expression, have different understandings of the relations between letters and sounds, and use a variety of resources to solve problems as they reflect on language and try to figure out how written language works. Computers can provide new ways to capture meaning that can enhance this reflection on language.

Using word-processing software that facilitates revision may help students reflect on language as well. Daiute (1988) describes how children can become absorbed in their writing, other people's perceptions of their writing, and the forms that their ideas take on the page or the computer screen. When a child is asked to revise, he or she often finds it difficult to do because once the text is written it becomes a fixed object. Revising is a complex process, but word-processing software makes the task easier than it is on paper. Therefore, children may be more likely to think about their writing and revise reflectively when this technology is available to them.

In Ms. Coltrane's classroom, students worked together as they revised their writing. The computer served as a tool that enhanced students' reflection on language. It helped students look at language and how they could use it to express meaning in multiple ways.

Rhett and Leonard are sharing a computer. Rhett is typing the final draft of Leonard's writing assignment concerning predictions for 1,000 years from now using *The Amazing Writing Machine.*

Rhett:	"I will predict that there will be flying cars." Is this your final draft?
Leonard:	No.
Rhett:	I predict that there will be flying cars that...that.... [Rhett pauses and waits for Leonard to suggest words to describe the flying cars. She types, *In a 1,000 years, I predict that their (sic) will be flying cars that make you go very fast*]
Rhett:	Do you need flying cars that make you go really fast? Comma, comma and... here, do you want to get that out of there? [Rhett points to a rectangular box for graphics in the middle of the text page.]
Leonard:	OK. [Rhett clicks on the box and erases it.]
Rhett:	Fast and...fly very high?
Leonard:	Yeah.

[Rhett types, *and fly very*]

Rhett:	H-i-.... Make you fly very high like a bird. How 'bout, like, make you soar?

Leonard: No. Fly very high. A different subject.

Rhett: Wait. A different paragraph. [Rhett asks Leonard for clarification.]

Leonard: When I'm....

Rhett: I'm?

Leonard: Yeah. [Rhett does not type what Leonard said, but instead types, *when I:*. Leonard begins to tell her about the correct punctuation.] That's semicolon. I'll find it. Just try this.

Rhett: I did. I did. [As Rhett repeats herself, she raises her voice.]

Leonard: That's it. You need a capital.

As they negotiated meanings using the different symbolic options available to them in the software, Rhett and Leonard reflected on form. They discussed changes, evaluated what was available in the software, argued with and corrected each other, offered suggestions to each other, and worked together to accomplish their social and intellectual goals of creating a final draft with peer support.

Reflection Point 2.3

Computers have the potential to help children understand the way that written language works. As Dyson (1989) explains, children need opportunities to grow not only as writers but also as users of varied media so that they may discover the interrelated purposes and power of all forms of expression.

1. Revisit the videotapes you created in Reflection Point 2.2 to find examples of how children made use of different symbol systems and how they reflected on the forms of language in their computer-based literacy activities. Record your observations in your journal.

2. Invite a colleague to view your videotape and discuss observations and insights on what each of you learned.

Computers in the Classroom: Where Do They Belong?

In every classroom, computers occupy a different space, and it is important to determine what role you want them to play in your classroom, what role your students want them to play, how they will be used to support your instructional goals, and how you will integrate them into your existing curriculum.

The Teacher's Perspective

Ms. Coltrane was interested in finding a way to use technology to support her instructional goals. She was open to learning both with and from her students, and she realized that incorporating technology into the literacy curriculum was a process that would be filled with challenges, mistakes, and opportunities. I interviewed Ms. Coltrane about this topic, and she shared her thoughts with me.

> Well, I think right now I really see it as a support tool for things that we're already doing, rather than having it be one more thing we have to teach. Of course, there are the skills and strategies that come along with using it, but I really, my goal is to try and implement it as seamlessly as possible into things we're already doing as a support tool. For example, with our independent research projects having it be used as a tool to do research. For literacy support during literacy centers and finding software that is compatible with that in all the curriculum areas is a challenge, too. Good quality software that's not just fill-in-the-blank drill and skill stuff. (personal communication, October 8, 1999)

Ms. Coltrane continually assessed the success and failure of computer use in her classroom as she experimented with different computer programs and Internet sites. She thought about how she could use computers to best support individual students and realized that different students used technology in different ways as they pursued their goals.

The Students' Perspectives

It was not uncommon for the students in Ms. Coltrane's class to gather around the computers each day in the moments after the hour-long literacy center time ended. Because everyone had an opportunity to participate in the computer activities at some point in the weekly rotations, the computers seemed to function as a highly visible shared reference that promoted communal chat. The children eagerly peered over each other's shoulders as they hoped to see what the students who had been using the computers during literacy center time had done and compare it with their own experiences. It seemed that everyone had something to say. Almost all the students in the room seemed to participate in this ritual each day, somewhat like an elementary school version of a coffee break. It seemed to be representative of their awareness of the importance and the presence of computers in the midst of their classroom lives.

For some students, computers provided a challenge, evoked competitive feelings, and served as a measure of performance. Many of the students were intent on "beating the level" in software programs such as *The Magic School Bus Explores the Ocean* (Scholastic, 1996) and *Reading Blaster* (Davidson, 1997). They had great fun as they did so.

Kelly: Go-go-go-go-go-go. We got one.

Brycen: Here I go. Look at those poor fish—they have a zero score. [Kelly and Brycen laugh hysterically as they frantically try to win the game by capturing fish.] Celebrate—oh fishie, fishie, survive—should I jump?

Kelly: We lose.

Brycen: We beat that guy at least, by 1 point. Wanna keep playing?

Kelly: Yes, yes!

Brycen: Hey, you guys, we're back at the little pool. This rocks! We're the best. Run for your life, little fishie!

Kelly: We only got 24; you're a stinkpot!

The game was motivating for the students, and they continued to explore different aspects of the program. Their goal was to win the game, yet they were discovering different kinds of information about the ocean environment as they played and explored.

For other students, such as Emma and Jill, computers served as a source of social bonding. They were friends playing as they worked together.

Emma:	Jilly, are you sure you don't want to play? Jilly, Jilly, Jilly, do you have it?
Jill:	What?
Emma:	The American Girl CD-ROM.
Jill:	There's Molly. I have Molly [one of the American Girl dolls]. [Jill points to the character as she appears on the screen.]

Oliver, too, described how he liked to work with his friends as he used computers: "All I do is, like, grab a friend. We just play.... I like a partner with me because, like, on math games, I could get help with something."

Sometimes computers motivated students to explore different facets of words, sounds, and graphics. For example, Serena was using word-processing software that allowed her to hear music as she typed. She delightedly tried various sounds. When she typed a random string of letters very quickly, she smiled and said, "I was just looking what it would sound like."

For many students, the interactive element of computer use was intriguing and motivating. Elena commented, "When you watch TV, you can't really do anything, but when you're on a computer it's like you get to do something, and you get, they tell you, like, what to do."

For others, fun and novelty were essential. Seth said, "I love playing computer games!" He said his favorites were the Magic School Bus games because "usually they've got a lot of stuff to do. You can drive a bus around something...sometimes you can explore the places. You can even go in the back of the bus."

It is important to consider your own perspective on computer use and ask your students to share their perspectives as you plan computer-based literacy activities. Throughout this book, we will learn about the literacy activities that occurred around the classroom computer as we try to gain insight into ways that teachers can find the "best place" for computers in their own particular classrooms.

Reflection Point 2.4

As computers are being used in more and more classrooms, it is helpful to examine technology from varied perspectives. Examine your own views and ideas regarding computer use. You also may want to engage in dialogue with your peers and explore professional resources, such as academic journals and conference presentations. Other important perspectives to examine are the history of technology in your school and your school district's philosophy on technology use. It is often helpful to have this information as you begin to make decisions about how to best incorporate technology into your own classroom. Ask the following questions:

What is the history of technology use in your school and your district?

What are the successes and failures that result from implementing technology in your school?

Who are the people in your school or district who are most influential in making decisions regarding technology use and materials in the classroom?

What can you do to foster communication among the different people who make use of technology throughout your school and district?

Chapter 3

"I'm Glad We Could All Put Our Heads Together": Voices and Values in the Classroom Community

At the end of each day, the students gather in a circle on the floor. Each student has a chance to comment on the day, raise concerns, ask questions, and share stories. One afternoon the class was discussing what happened when Rhett was excluded from a play that her classmates were creating.

Rhett:	*I felt bad that all the girls are putting on a play and I can't be in it.*
Ms. Coltrane:	*I really appreciate you sharing it. Can you be more specific?*
Analia:	*Some people said that Rhett could be in it and some said she couldn't.*
Ms. Coltrane:	*Let's talk about it.*
Emma and Ruby:	*We let her in...at the end.*
Serena:	*Yesterday we said no to not let Rhett play 'cause we didn't know if Jo was gonna be here.*
Ms. Coltrane:	*Put yourself in Rhett's position. If you were the only one who wasn't in a play and all the other girls were.... Ruby asked me if we should let Rhett play. Say she chose not to. What do we do in class? Do we not have math centers if there is an odd number?*
Emma:	*So there's five instead of four.*

Ms. Coltrane:	*In my opinion, someone's feelings are a lot more important than having an even number. Does anyone have any suggestions?*
Ruby:	*We let her in this morning. We were thinking about it after school.*
Ms. Coltrane:	*What could we have done yesterday?*
Analia:	*We, we, could just have all the girls in it and we could just practice one more time.*
Serena:	*She could be an elf with Elena.*
Oliver:	*We could change the parts.*
Ms. Coltrane:	*I'm glad we could all put our heads together.*

The Classroom Community

This vignette illustrates an important part of Ms. Coltrane's classroom environment: building a classroom community in which each student's feelings are respected. Ms. Coltrane tried to foster a sense of community in the classroom by making the group responsible for individual problems, by explicitly stating her own beliefs about respecting others, and by sharing the responsibility for creating this environment with her students.

It is important to determine the values that are a part of our own classroom because they create the context in which learning happens. The classroom community is created by teachers' expectations for learning, for student behavior, and for how students talk to the teacher and to each other, and it is shaped and changed by the teacher and the students as each day unfolds. Looking closely at the components of our own classroom community can help us learn more about our own values and how best to support our students' learning. As Freedman (1994) states, teachers who are best suited to responding to the needs of diverse individuals are those most able to create a sense of community in their classrooms.

Reflection Point 3.1

Classroom communities are defined in many ways. A classroom community may be defined by something as simple as whether or not it is OK to borrow a pencil sitting on a desk or by how much choice you feel comfortable giving students in selecting what book to read.

1. Write down four or five specific descriptions that you feel illustrate your classroom community.

2. What do you value most in your classroom?

3. How can you create a classroom community that supports your values?

4. Discuss your responses with a colleague.

In this chapter, we will explore Ms. Coltrane's classroom community and how technology was nested within it. We also will learn more about the classroom literacy curriculum and the voices and values that shaped it. The most important issue central to understanding the role of technology in literacy development is that it must be viewed as a tool that children use as they engage in social and intellectual work in the context of the existing classroom community. Technology did not produce this community; instead, it introduced new possibilities for meaning-making into it.

Literacy Centers

As we explore what occurred during the different literacy activities, we see how the teacher's voice and the students' voices embody classroom values. As previously mentioned, Ms. Coltrane's literacy curriculum was organized around a series of reading and writing activities called literacy centers. These were stations set up around the classroom, and each day the students spent time in a specific literacy center. The activities in the literacy centers always included computers (when there were no computer hardware or software problems). Other activities included Word Works, a word analysis program that was usually run by an adult volunteer; handwriting; one-on-one reading; book clubs in which students who were reading the same book met individually or in groups of two or three to discuss and answer questions; and the writing of essays, poems, research reports, and book reviews. Some of the projects that students focused on during the course of the study included writing tall tales, research reports on the ocean, and research reports on Americans who made a difference. The use of computers was not an add-on to the literacy curriculum; rather, it was an established activity that students looked forward to. Ms. Coltrane looked for software and websites to support her literacy instruction. She also used the computers as research resources, and she encouraged the students to explore.

In order to understand the literacy curriculum, it is important to look closely at the underlying values that supported it and composed the classroom community. Six key classroom norms characterized the classroom community that Ms. Coltrane cocreated with her students:

1. a focus on process

2. the centrality of choice

3. a critical stance toward information sources

4. using one another as resources

5. a supportive risk-taking environment

6. caring, respect, and responsibility for others as members of a learning community

These norms represent values that defined the classroom community and were embodied in the consistent behaviors and expectations. The norms are the basis of what is important in the classroom. Each of these norms contributed in different ways to shape a community within which the students were empowered agents in their own learning.

A Focus on Process

The students in Ms. Coltrane's classroom were in an environment in which process was stressed above product. They were encouraged to think about what they were doing and how they were doing it. For example, in an interview Ms. Coltrane talked about how it may have been easier for the students to revise on the computer in their first research report of the school year but she wanted them to complete their revisions by hand so that she could see the process and adjust her teaching accordingly.

The students worked on their ocean research projects for nearly four weeks. At the same time that they were working on their individual projects, they also created a class project through which Ms. Coltrane was able to model all the steps involved in a research project. Teacher modeling allowed students to gain more in-depth knowledge of a variety of concepts, develop research and writing skills, and view learning as an incremental process. Students had direct instruction on each step of the process that they then could use as a guide in creating their individual projects. (See Figure 3 for an example of how to model the writing process.)

Figure 3
Modeling the Writing Process

1. Brainstorming Ideas: Ms. Coltrane asked students questions such as What interests you about this topic? and Have you ever heard ideas about this topic? and discussed their answers. She then wrote students' ideas on the board. To further stimulate students, you can show them images related to the writing topic or read them passages on the topic.

2. Think-Alouds and Collecting Facts: Ms. Coltrane asked the students to write each fact they had collected about a topic on a strip of paper. She then read aloud each fact and modeled the thought process one would go through to decide whether the fact was useful and where it should be categorized.

3. Creating Organizers: Ms. Coltrane placed the facts that the students collected in an organizer. As more and more facts were collected, the class modified the categories. Ms. Coltrane showed the students how to use the organizer to help them write their first draft. First, she chose a fact, then she modeled how to write a sentence incorporating the fact, and finally she added more facts to create a coherent paragraph.

4. Drafting and Invented Spelling: Ms. Coltrane wrote a first draft on the board. She talked as she wrote, crossed out items, and rewrote frequently. She told her students that a draft was a first copy, not a finished product, and that it was intended to help a writer get ideas down on paper. She reminded the students that invented spelling, where the words are often approximations of correct spelling, is acceptable in a first draft.

5. Editing and Publishing: Ms. Coltrane explained to the students that in order for something to be published, it must be free of errors, including spelling and punctuation errors. She showed students how to edit their drafts and held one-on-one conferences to help students edit.

In an interview, Ms. Coltrane said,

> We go through that whole process from beginning to end as a class first as a model. And I'm trying to kind of stay one step ahead of them, but at the same time the students are either in groups or individually taking it through that very same process on their own. So they're getting the actual practice of having to find resources for research, having to [gather] information and synthesizing, develop those facts, and write the report. Whereas in a more traditional classroom it may not be quite as in depth and as involved and it may in fact...it may just be, "here are your books—read them—write a book report on an ocean animal." It's just there's a lot more depth to it, and I think the emphasis is much more on process. (personal communication, October 8, 1999)

Writing individual research projects involved using a variety of resources. Students used books they found in the school library and on the classroom shelves. The classroom computers were integral research tools. Ms. Coltrane taught minilessons on how to use the Yahooligans search engine. Students often found information on other students' topics during their Internet research and eagerly shared what they had found. Students also were taught how to organize the facts that they collected.

The following description of a writing activity illustrates another aspect of how process was emphasized in this classroom. Ms. Coltrane had two goals for her students in the activity. First, she wanted the students to become aware of their writing by focusing on several important features of writing. These features included the use of details; "wow" words (highly descriptive words); imaginative capabilities; capitalization, punctuation, and spelling; flow and focus on topic; neatness (in a final draft); the beginning, middle, and end of stories; problem and solution aspects; trials and errors in a story; grabbers (to draw the reader in); showing, not telling, words that paint a picture; and description that captured sensory images and ideas. Her second goal was to develop a class writing rubric.

To meet the first goal, Ms. Coltrane had the students revisit the tall tales they had written several weeks prior.

Ms. Coltrane: Now that it's been a while, I want you to read your own tall tale. [Ms. Coltrane gave each student two sticky notes.] On one sticky note write *GLOW* and the other *GROW*. After you reread your tall tales, use the

GLOW sticky note to list the things that you did well in your writing and the GROW note to list what you want to improve in your writing. What are some things that make a great tall tale?

[The class discusses several of the attributes of tall tales.]

In this activity, Ms. Coltrane modeled for students how to revisit their own writing and focus on the process. She explained the difference between saying things such as "Great job" versus "I really like the way you used different specific 'wow' words." She suggested specific examples such as "I really liked the grabber you used at the beginning to draw someone in," and "Next time I'm going to have the flow of my idea better." The students then took the time to focus on their own writing because they had to look at it with fresh eyes and as a new task before them.

The students had some insightful comments about how they both "glowed" and could "grow."

Rhett wrote, "It could have more things that are true in it.... More wow words."

Seth thought he could have "more use of show not tell." He thought he made "good use of wow words."

Emma thought she could have made her tall tale longer but that she had used a lot of imagination (see Figure 4 for an example of Emma's glow and grow writing).

Analia thought that she needed a grabber and that she did well on exaggerations.

Serena thought she had great pictures. On the GROW sticky note, she wrote, "I could write more details because I left out details."

Elena wrote "creativity" on her GLOW sticky note. She also thought she needed to clarify her tale and add more trials for her character.

Perhaps the most striking evidence of the focus on process occurred one day shortly before the Thanksgiving holiday when Ms. Coltrane said that she had some Dittos for the students to work on. Serena looked at her with a puzzled expression and asked, "What's a Ditto?" For these students, the ubiquitous Ditto that defines "product" in so many classrooms was an anomaly because they rarely used them.

Figure 4
Emma's Glow and Grow Writing

The Centrality of Choice

When Ms. Coltrane described her classroom in an interview, she said that there was "an openness and a freedom to make choices, to have responsibility..." (personal communication, October 8, 1999). This was evident in the classroom as students were given varied and numerous opportunities to make choices as they moved through daily activities. This focus on choice carried over to students' use of the computers. Students had the freedom to make choices and mistakes as they experimented with computers during literacy center time. One of the greatest strengths of computers as a learning tool in this classroom was that they provided multiple options for students to explore different software programs and Internet links. These students were familiar with making choices although different students had different comfort levels with choice. Overall, choice was a central element of the classroom community, and it was very important to Ms. Coltrane.

Ms. Coltrane often used students' choices as a way to monitor the students' own understandings and assessments of their abilities. For example, during a morning math activity, Ms. Coltrane wrote three examples on the board that varied in difficulty levels. She told the students to choose one to work on. She said, "I want to see if you're able to make a decision about your own learning."

Ms. Coltrane respected the students' choices as well. When Oliver was struggling with how to figure out what combination of blocks to use to make a number, Ms. Coltrane asked him, "Would you like some help, or would you like to try and continue to figure it out for yourself?"

He answered, "Himself."

When the class was reading the book *The Polar Express* (Van Allsburg, 1985), Ms. Coltrane relayed that when she was a student, she had been in a play based on the book. She said she had kept the book since then and it was her favorite book. "But that is my opinion," she pointed out. "You can think the book is boring."

Ms. Coltrane felt that choices were important not only in school but also in life. In an interview she said,

> A day never goes exactly as you have it planned in your mind, you know.
> So I tell the kids, too, if it's not working for you and you can't get help from
> someone and I'm busy, then you know what other choices are good choic-

es to make and we have to deal with that. That's a life skill. Sometimes things don't go our way and you have to be flexible. (personal communication, October 8, 1999)

As these examples show, choice was a central norm that permeated the instructional and social climate of this classroom.

Reflection Point 3.2

In most busy classrooms, there are not many opportunities for students to make choices. It is important, however, to help students develop this skill. When opportunities do arise, talk to your students about how you make choices, and provide models on how to make effective choices. To help students become independent decision makers, provide opportunities for them to make their own choices. This can involve asking the students to select a book to read during free reading time, allowing them to decide what computer software program to explore during free time, or asking them to select a classmate to be the leader of the lunch line.

1. What role does choice play in your curriculum? How important do you feel student choice is?

2. Over the course of a week, try to provide 10 opportunities for your students to make choices in daily classroom life. Record your observations.

3. Reflect on how increasing students' opportunities to make choices affected your learning goals.

A Critical Stance Toward Information Sources

Through teacher modeling and commentary, Ms. Coltrane encouraged her students to take a critical stance toward information sources and to challenge the authority implicit in them. This stance was particularly help-ful to the students as they worked on computers because they often en-countered contradictory information on the Internet. The students were comfortable challenging resources.

One morning the students were reading a chart that described the food chain in the ocean. According to the chart, the leopard fish only ate one thing. Ms. Coltrane said, "I have a problem with this resource," mak-ing it clear to the students that it was quite acceptable to challenge a print resource.

Another time, Analia was reading information on a website. She told Ms. Coltrane that, according to the website, "There are five layers in the ocean." Previously, though, the students had read different information from another source. Ms. Coltrane said, "So we have conflicting re-sources?" This is important to acknowledge because students often will find conflicting information as they use the computers for information.

Using One Another as Resources

The social organization of Ms. Coltrane's classroom often required that children make use of one another as resources during computer-based lit-eracy activities. These interactions are essential. As Langer (1987) states, learners who assume ownership for their literacy activities gain control of their own abilities as literate thinkers and doers, and use language to serve their own needs. As students question, challenge, and discuss ideas with other students, they become active users of language with specific goals.

Leu and Leu (1999) state that socially mediated learning is central to success with using computers in the classroom. In this student-centered classroom, Ms. Coltrane encouraged the children to use one another as resources because she did not view herself as the source of all knowledge. In an informal interview she said, "I'm not the expert on everything. We're all learning from resources" (personal communication, October 27, 1999).

Ms. Coltrane often encouraged asking a peer for help, and this was a classroom norm with which the students were comfortable. As Ms. Coltrane introduced the literacy centers the class would be using one morning, she said,

If you can't remember, call on a friend to help you. The literacy center pocket chart tells where you go. In the Internet center, you can have a third grader buddy read to a second grader. If you need help writing, ask a friend! It's always OK to ask for help. (personal communication, September 30, 1999)

When Ms. Coltrane was explaining to the class how to begin finding information about their subjects for biographies by using the different search engines on the computer, she asked the students, "If you are not familiar [with the search engines], who could you ask?" One student suggested asking the aide. Ms. Coltrane, however, said, "We have some experts here in the group," reminding them to use one another as resources for learning.

Another example of students using one another as resources occurred one day after the students had been working in small groups writing their individual tall tales. Ms. Coltrane interrupted them and asked, "Does anyone have a good beginning they would like to read to the class?" Several students stood and read what they had written thus far. In making time to share their work, Ms. Coltrane encouraged the students to use one another as sources for inspiration in writing.

Ms. Coltrane also facilitated students' use of one another as resources by allowing them to answer questions for themselves. For example, one morning, the students were discussing ways to improve their writing.

Oliver: Well, it's sort of on to Joey's blah-de-blah-de-blah Paul Bunyan made, blah-de-blah—also he had a friend—blah-de-blah. You can say a sentence about the character and then you can say, like, like, say, um, you just told a sentence about the character and then you would tell, like, his friend, and blah, his friend, was also helpful, too. [Ms. Coltrane does not intervene. Instead, she simply waits. Two other students begin asking Oliver questions.]

Oliver: I'm talking about flow. Tell, like, in your story, you would tell a sentence about the character, then in the next sentence you would also say, his friend would also help him.

By validating the students' expertise, acknowledging her own limitations, and facilitating peer mentoring, Ms. Coltrane encouraged students to use one another as information resources in this classroom.

Reflection Point 3.3

Encouraging students to use one another as resources involves being willing to share authority with your students and validating the knowledge that each person has in varied areas. Moll (1994) describes funds of knowledge, which are knowledge and skills that varied individuals and groups possess and share with others.

1. Ask your students to answer the following questions and remind them to include academic and nonacademic knowledge in their answers:

   What topic do you know a lot about?

   What do you consider yourself an expert on?

   What skill can you share with your classmates?

2. Collect the students' responses, and create a class chart titled "Funds of Knowledge" that summarizes all the knowledge and skills that your students possess.

3. Ask the students to collect information about the expertise in their own families and communities. You may wish to add this information to your class chart. Emphasize the fact that students and teachers are able to learn many different things by using others as resources.

A Supportive Risk-Taking Environment

Risk-taking is a difficult skill to develop for all learners. It is based on trust. In this classroom, students were encouraged to take risks. Ms. Coltrane explicitly and publicly supported those who did. For example, one day she asked the students, who were just learning to tell time, to guess how much time was left until recess. Someone ventured an incorrect guess, and Ms. Coltrane said, "That's OK. We're learning. Thanks for taking a risk."

Another example of encouraging students to take risks occurred one day as the class had just finished a brief partner activity. Oliver said that he had not been able to find a partner. Someone suggested asking people, and Ms. Coltrane asked, "Oliver, did you hear that suggestion? Ask a group of two if you can become a group of three? You can stand up and ask who needs a partner. That's taking a risk."

Ms. Coltrane used students' ideas, gave direct feedback as to how to go about risk-taking, characterized the inherent difficulties in doing so, and supported students' risk-taking efforts in the classroom. The students' comfort levels regarding risk-taking became evident in the ways they made use of technology as well. Much of initial computer use involves risk-taking, as users wonder what will happen as they experiment with the mouse and the keyboard. Ms. Coltrane's students had different comfort levels with risk-taking, yet they worked within a classroom environment that supported and valued it.

Reflection Point 3.4

Encouraging students to take risks is an important part of their development as literacy learners. It can be as simple as encouraging them to use the context to figure out the meaning of an unfamiliar word or supporting their guesses when you ask a difficult question.

1. Audiotape three class discussions. Analyze student–teacher interactions, and look for examples when you encouraged or discouraged risk-taking behaviors.

2. Implement strategies to encourage risk-taking with your students. Involve them in the process. At the end of each day, as a class, take time to reflect on examples of risk-taking behaviors. When students see how you value this skill, it will become an increasingly valued and important part of your classroom community.

Caring, Respect, and Responsibility for Others as Members of a Learning Community

Creating a community of caring, respect, and responsibility for others is a difficult and complex effort. In an informal interview, Ms. Coltrane said that she saw her class as a "community" and the class was "connected to her and to each other." There was an understanding developed in the classroom that an individual's problem would become the group's problem to solve. Ms. Coltrane developed this community by taking the time to discuss issues that were important to students, asking them for suggestions on how to solve problems, clearly articulating her feelings about different issues that arose in everyday classroom life, and sharing the responsibility for creating this environment with students. It was in this environment of support that technology use occurred.

In Your Classroom

The values reflected in Ms. Coltrane's classroom were important to her. How can you use what you have learned about her classroom community to support technology integration in your own classroom? Learning about what you value is an important part of making decisions about how to use computers in the literacy curriculum.

For example, a focus on process is important in technology integration. If students are used to completing short, drill-like exercises, they may be uncomfortable with both the persistence and the skills needed to undertake Internet-based research. Providing time and support and valuing student efforts in these endeavors is critical. The difficulty often lies in finding a balance between accomplishment of tasks and the time needed to engage in the process of learning while using computers. For example, if you have given students the opportunity to conduct Internet research, you might want to take time to assess its success by discussing and evaluating the process with them.

The centrality of choice in a curriculum involves a willingness to share authority with your students. Cambourne and Turbill (1987) describe the importance of learner responsibility for independence and self-direction as a vital part of optimal learning conditions in the classroom. You have to determine parameters for choice, as well as think about your own comfort level. A good way to introduce this element in your classroom is to begin with providing students with a choice between one or two options, and then gradually increasing the amount of individual responsibility for choice as time goes on.

Making choices is a vital component of computer use. You might want to conduct a lesson to show students how different choices are available to them as they use particular software or conduct Internet research. For example, you might investigate a new software program together and show the students how different navigational choices lead you to different places in the program. As Metsala (1996) states,

> Building choice of reading topics and materials into the reading instructional program is an important way to help children's individual interests and curiosity develop through their reading, as is allowing children opportunities to interact with others about their reading. Using computers widens the range of choice available to students. (p. 362)

Teaching your students how to develop a critical stance toward information sources and challenge the authority implicit in them also is essential to computer use in the classroom. Information on diverse topics is widely available on the Internet, and computers bring the voices of many experts into the classroom. As a result, we must assist students in becoming more critical consumers of the information they encounter (Alvermann, Moon, & Hagood, 1999). This is a distinct change from a time when textbooks were a main source of information in classrooms.

A good exercise to develop students' ability to take a critical stance is to create a class rubric based on an analysis of a variety of Internet sites. Include the author of the site, the credibility of the author, the kinds of information provided, the links suggested, and comparisons to other sources of information. Box 3.1 contains resources for evaluating websites, including sample rubrics that may be helpful.

As evidenced in Ms. Coltrane's classroom, students and teachers can learn from one another as technology users. One of the greatest benefits of Internet technology is that the teacher is no longer the sole "owner" of content knowledge. In addition, students often have expertise in different aspects of computer use. For example, one student might know how to insert a disk or load a program, and another might know a good search

---

Box 3.1
Resources for Evaluating Websites

Evaluating Websites: Criteria and Tools
www.library.cornell.edu/okuref/research/webeval.html

Evaluation Rubrics for Websites
www.siec.k12.in.us/~west/online/eval.htm

Teaching Students to Evaluate Internet Information Critically
www.readingonline.org/editorial/edit_index.asp?HREF=december2001/index.html

Yahooligans Teacher Guide
www.yahooligans.com/tg/evaluatingwebsites.html

---

engine to use. Encourage your students to share their knowledge so they can learn from one another. One way to encourage your students to share their knowledge is by hosting a Computer Expert Day in your classroom on the last day of each month. At the beginning of each month, brainstorm a list of problems students may be having with the computers and things they would like to learn more about. Encourage students to add topics to the list as further questions arise throughout the month. Assign or ask for volunteers to research one of the topics and create a presentation for their classmates that addresses the topic. Invite other classes to attend the Computer Expert Day sessions.

Risk-taking is essential to learning. As you encourage your students to become increasingly independent learners, it is important to support their efforts. You can model effective questioning techniques, show your students how to use a wide range of strategies to solve problems, and talk about the risks you take as a learner. Some students may feel that if they press the wrong button the computer will not work correctly; therefore, it is important for you and your students to feel comfortable with the knowledge that as you take risks and make mistakes, you also will take the initiative to solve problems as they arise. The open-ended nature of computer use challenges learners who are accustomed to a more structured learning experience, and different students have different levels of comfort with risk. This knowledge can be helpful in informing your instructional goals. Use what you know about your students to help them become successful risk-takers.

Your students have opportunities to communicate with a wide range of people as they use computers. You can assist them in finding Internet pen pals, learning how different people live and what they think about the world, and opening their minds to diverse viewpoints as you integrate new learning experiences into the literacy curriculum. You can foster an awareness of respect for others and promote a sense of global responsibility as your students learn about the world through computer explorations. Leu (1999) describes the important role technology can play in facilitating communication and enriching one's understanding of diverse cultures. Box 3.2 contains examples of global Internet resources.

Ms. Coltrane and her students cocreated a community in which many voices were heard. With this discussion of classroom community as a backdrop, we can begin to explore more fully in the following chapters the students' collaborations, explorations, and play in computer-based literacy events.

BOX 3.2
Global Internet Resources

Disability Social History Project
www.disabilityhistory.org/dshp.html

Multicultural Pavilion
http://curry.edschool.virginia.edu/go/multicultural

World Peace Project for Children
www.sadako.org

---

*Reflection Point 3.5*_____

1. What did you find to be the most compelling part of Ms. Coltrane's classroom community? Why?

2. Note your own observations and reflections on how your instructional efforts reflect the values that are important to you.

Create a list of specific incidents when your instruction was compatible with your values. Exchange your list with a colleague and discuss.

3. How can technology be used to enhance your instructional goals and support your classroom values? Create a lesson that you believe will be helpful in these two areas. Implement the lesson. Critique and evaluate the lesson after you have taught it. What did you learn?

Chapter 4

Cooperating Classmates and Colliding Friends: Computer Collaborations

Emma and Joshua are working together using the computer program
The Magic School Bus Explores the Ocean *(Scholastic, 1996), based
on the book series by Joanna Cole. The students are exploring an option
that allows them to change the facial features of characters.*

> Emma: How about her mouth?
>
> Joshua: No!
>
> Emma: I don't like that one either. [The next option appears on the
> screen.] Yeah, yeah, I like that one.
>
> Joshua: OK, hit Save.
>
> Emma: OK, let's try—I like that, that, that, she's brown lady. Do
> you like that or do you like brown? [Emma varies the
> character's skin color by dragging a bar that controls the
> intensity.]
>
> Joshua: I like brown better.

In this chapter, we will explore the nature of children's collaborative efforts in the accomplishment of social and intellectual work in the classroom. Understanding the ways in which children develop as literacy learners as they participate in collaborative events becomes critical as more and more students spend time working together at the computer, and the teacher, although setting clear instructional goals, becomes less visible. As these things happen, interactions among students come to play a key role in literacy learning because the people one learns with influence what and how one learns.

Vygotsky (1934/1978, 1934/1986) has helped illuminate the social dimensions of learning and emphasized the importance of understanding language as a vital part of intellectual development. Education researchers and practitioners have developed many models and approaches to cooperative and collaborative learning (Bruffee, 1993; Cohen, 1986, 1994; Johnson & Johnson, 1987; Kagan, 1990; Slavin, 1983). The focus of these approaches includes restructuring classroom tasks and instructional strategies and capitalizing on the dynamic social dimensions of learning.

In peer collaborative efforts in the classroom, students negotiate meaning (Ruddell & Unrau, 1994). Molinelli (2000) suggests that the type and quality of group interactions ultimately determine the nature and degree of any cognitive and social benefit for students. This is especially true as students work together in multimedia environments. As Leu (1996) states, "[L]earning is frequently constructed through social interactions in these contexts, perhaps even more naturally and frequently than in traditional print environments" (p. 163).

Much of the work that occurred around Ms. Coltrane's classroom computer was collaborative, as students shared four computers while participating in small-group literacy activities. Ms. Coltrane had given the students a great deal of responsibility for figuring out not only how the computers worked but also how to work together on them. She could not monitor every interaction, nor would she be inclined to do so.

Students responded differently to this freedom. Some were thrilled, and others were intimidated by the challenge. Some collaborative efforts were successful, and others were not. Students had different levels of social comfort depending on their partners. They were more or less assertive, silly, serious, or challenging, depending on whom they were sitting next to. They were quite comfortable with grabbing the mouse from some students, while with other students they were more timid. Different levels of expertise were important as well because knowledge of how to do something on the computer gave some students power in directing the collaboration.

*Reflection Point 4.1*_____

Collaboration is a complex process. It involves talking and nego-tiating and can be both productive and disruptive. It is impor-tant to examine your own comfort level with collaborative efforts in your classroom.

1. What are your thoughts regarding collaboration among the students in your classroom?

2. Do students feel comfortable asking one another for assistance?

3. Do you feel comfortable having the students use one another as resources? Why or why not?

4. Over the course of a week, collect examples of students asking for assistance. As you review your data, examine the different ways that students asked for help and how others responded.

5. How do you think the ways that students collaborate in your classroom may affect your planning and implementation of computer-based literacy activities?

Emma and Joshua: An Equitable Partnership

Sometimes collaborative efforts appeared to be equitable partnerships, where control of the direction of the event shifted between the partners. This became evident when Emma and Joshua collaborated as they worked with *The Magic School Bus Explores the Ocean* software. In the pro-gram, a classroom science teacher named Ms. Frizzle takes her class on a series of adventures involving the natural world. Users can hunt for hid-den treasure by following clues that lead them through different ocean zones. Users also have the opportunity to play games and do science ex-periments as they explore the ocean environment.

A warm, friendly tone permeated Emma and Joshua's interactions. They were friendly competitors and friendly collaborators, and their relationship was defined by the easy comfort of knowing that one could have the power to control the computer mouse and navigation at one moment, and that they could and would be able to change back and forth between these roles at any given time. Emma viewed herself as Joshua's equal and was quite comfortable telling him what to do, challenging him, and engaging in moment-to-moment power struggles with him.

At times Emma and Joshua shared the mouse equitably. During the following interaction, Joshua has the mouse and Emma puts her hand over his. They try to move the school bus that appears on the screen closer to the edge of the sea (see Figure 5).

Joshua: See if we can go in the water. [Emma takes the mouse from him. They look at each other and laugh when Emma's turn ends and a new scene appears.]

Emma: I'm all wah wah.... [Emma mimics crying.]

Joshua: Your turn.

Figure 5
Screen From *The Magic School Bus Explores the Ocean*

From *The Magic School Bus Explores the Ocean Floor* by Joanna Cole, illustrated by Bruce Degen. Text copyright 1996 by Joanna Cole, illustrations copyright 1996 by Bruce Degen. Used by permission of Scholastic Inc. The Magic School Bus is a registered trademark of Scholastic Inc.

Emma and Joshua also fought over the mouse, and whoever got a hand on it seemed to be the one in control. In the following example, Joshua tries to grab the mouse from Emma.

Emma: No! Let me see! Oh! A diving board. What are we supposed to do?

Joshua: I know. [Joshua quickly grabs the mouse away from Emma.]

They also made joint decisions such as when they played with an option that allowed them to vary the physical traits of the character they created.

Emma: I want to see. [She drags down the bar to change the skin tone of their character.]

Joshua: I don't care. You do it.

Emma: Oh, my gosh, look at the nose! I don't like the nose. [She changes the nose.] There, that's better.

Joshua: I like that.

Emma: I guess that one's OK. That one's OK. I'm gonna look here again. I don't like that one.

Joshua: Either do I.

This collaborative effort was characterized by ongoing shifts of power, as Emma and Joshua each took and gave up control at different times. Power was a flexible and dynamic entity that was enacted in the context of a collaborative relationship. This example illustrates that how a child constructs meaning in a literacy event is influenced by who he or she is working with.

Reflection Point 4.2 _____

In order to create effective collaborative partnerships it is important to reflect on how your students work together in a variety of situations.

1. Respond to the following prompts:

If I were to select pairs of students most likely to be effective collaborators, I would choose _____.

If I were to select pairs of students least likely to be effective collaborators, I would choose _____.

If I were to select groups of three or four students most likely to be effective collaborators, I would choose _____.

If I were to select groups of three or four students least likely to be effective collaborators, I would choose _____.

2. Over the course of a two-week period, group students according to the choices you have made. Record your observations about the selections you made. What did you learn? What surprised you? What information can you use to inform your future instructional planning?

Emma and Serena: A Collision of Differences

A different result of collaboration, one characterized by a collision of differences, became apparent as Emma and Serena worked together. Ms. Coltrane had asked the students to work at a website featuring the author of the Harry Potter book series, J.K. Rowling. The students' task was to read the author's interview on the website, answer questions based on the interview, and record their answers in their reading journals. Ms. Coltrane wrote the following information on the whiteboard near the computers:

Open bookmark: New York Times Bestseller List
(www.scholastic.com/harrypotter/jkinterview.htm)

Click on *Chamber of Secrets*.

Click on author J.K. Rowling.

Click on her photograph. Read the interview.

Answer in your reading journal (complete sentences!).

1. What can you expect to see in the future of Harry Potter?

2. What does J.K. like about being an author?

3. If you had the chance to interview J.K., what would you ask her?

As they began their work, Emma struggled to read and understand the words on the website. At first, she seemed unaware that she was reading a transcript of an author interview.

Emma: She wrote this book?

Serena does not answer Emma and quickly begins to read in a soft voice and makes comments under her breath. Ms. Coltrane intervenes.

Emma: I can't read it.

Ms. Coltrane: How about reading it aloud? How are we going to do it? Emma, how about if you ask Serena—

Emma: I would like you to read it to me.

Ms. Coltrane: Serena, as an older reading buddy you would get some practice with your expression. [Serena complies with Ms. Coltrane's request. She explains the interview format used on the website to Emma.]

Serena: The yellow is the question and the white is her. [Emma, with a confused expression, looks back at Ms. Coltrane, who is walking away.]

Serena: Listen to me! [Serena continues to read aloud the rest of the information. She is a fast and fluent reader. Emma asks several questions. Serena does not answer. When Serena finishes reading, the girls take out their reading journals. Serena writes out the author's name for Emma in her journal. Emma does not begin writing.]

Serena: Remember, I read it to you. You got to write down what you think it is!

Emma: I can't read this—what am I supposed to do?

Serena: Oh, geez!

In this collaboration, all the elements of a successful collaboration were in place. A more fluent and less fluent reader were paired, and an older student read aloud difficult text to a younger student. The problem arose within the social relationship between the girls. Serena was a confident third grader who had little patience for those who could not keep her pace. She had both the expertise and control of the mouse. Emma was a shy, uncertain second grader who knew she was not getting the information she needed, but she did not know how to ask for help. The girls were frustrated by the result of their efforts.

Reflection Point 4.3

1. How might you have responded had you observed this collaboration? Would you have intervened in a different way? Why or why not?

2. What do you think Serena thought about this collaboration? What do you think Emma's perception of the collaboration was?

Ms. Coltrane realized that she had to monitor the collaborations more closely. She had set up what appeared to be a fruitful collaboration but realized that her students needed more modeling on how to effectively work together. She also realized that becoming an effective collaborator was not something that students could learn in a brief lesson but would develop over the course of the school year.

Reflection Point 4.4

1. Begin an ongoing journal log of "collaborative collisions" in your classroom. Include the following:

   Who had a difference of opinion?

   What did they disagree about?

   How was the difference resolved?

2. Reflect on your observations and brainstorm ways to help your students learn to effectively resolve disagreements and collaborate more effectively.

3. Discuss your ideas and share your insights with a colleague.

Analia and Jo: A Mutual Delight

Collaboration between a more knowledgeable partner and a less knowledgeable partner was not always characterized by dissonance. When Analia and Jo worked together on the same Internet activity that Serena and Emma had worked on, collaboration was not characterized by a collision of differences, but rather by a mutual and delightful effort.

As soon as they began, Analia directed Jo.

Analia: Click on, OK, click on author J.K. Rowlings. J.K. Rowling. Let's see. Where's J.K. Rowlings?

Jo: What are we supposed to do?

Analia: [in a kind voice] I just said. [Analia looks up at the white board.]

Jo: How... I think we're supposed to read this. [Analia takes the time to monitor Jo's understanding of what she is reading aloud.]

Analia: Does that make sense? What are you doing? Are you listening?

Jo: Yeah. [Analia realizes that the reading is difficult to understand, and she begins pointing to each word on the screen with her pencil as she reads aloud.]

Analia: Do you get it?

Jo: Kind of.... [Analia keeps reading aloud.]

Analia: Man-uuuss-ccriiii.... [She stumbles over the word *manuscript*. She reads the next question on the website.]

Analia: Cas... Do you know what that is? [They read further.]

Analia: Do you want to read now?

Jo: No. [Analia continues to read.]

Analia took the lead in creating an effective partnership. She monitored her own learning and Jo's learning in pursuit of their shared goal. Because the atmosphere that defined the relationship was fun and supportive, their shared goal was mutually attainable. Although Analia was aware that Jo was not as fluent a reader as she was, she acted in such a way as to make Jo comfortable with this situation. Analia did not seem to view herself as an expert but invited Jo to use her as a resource because she was able to see herself as someone from whom her peer could learn.

The girls were motivated to read about a favorite class author on the computer. This website also provided them with access to written language and graphics that gave them information about J.K. Rowling. They manipulated these different symbol systems as they navigated through the website and planned, talked about, and thought about what they were doing. During this friendly and supportive collaboration, they used the tool of technology to pursue their goals. In this collaborative effort affective elements were critical because the social relationship between the girls was key to the success of the collaboration.

In all the vignettes, the computer afforded students opportunities to use multiple symbol systems—such as language and graphics—and the opportunity to manipulate objects and navigate through program options. Affective elements such as fun, frustration, delight, harmony, and cooperation permeated their efforts. The students learned much about collaboration as they constructed meaning in the context of social relationships.

Reflection Point 4.5

Do you notice that some students seem to have more power or influence in your classroom than other students? Sometimes this comes from students' social status, expertise, personal style, or a desire to help others.

1. It is often easier to observe students' interactions during nonacademic tasks or nonacademic settings, such as during snack time or on the playground. Set aside time to observe your students and to try to identify their nonacademic interactions and how they might affect collaborative efforts in your classroom. Keep an ongoing record of your observations. This information might include who students play with, what choices they make, and how they resolve conflicts. Reflect on your observations and answer the following questions:

   How did your observations help you gain insight into students' relationships?

   What did you learn?

How can you use what you have learned to enhance your instructional goals?

2. List three specific goals that you will implement to foster collaboration in your classroom.

3. Revisit some of your observations from Reflection Point 1.2 and
reflect on what you have learned.

In Your Classroom

How can you use what you have learned about collaboration in Ms.
Coltrane's classroom to enhance your own instruction? Children's responses to one another's symbolic acts imbue those acts with social
meaning (Dyson, 1993). For example, students with good relationships,
like Emma and Joshua's, are able to effectively collaborate. They had a
sense of equality in their relationship that furthered their collaborative
efforts. This ease allowed them the comfort of exploring together, and
their meaning-making efforts were fruitful. It is important to look closely
at the social interactions among the students in your classroom. You can
use your nonacademic observations to inform your instruction as you plan
collaborative computer-based literacy activities.

Hartup (1996) describes how friendship interactions are more equitable
and positive, more task oriented, and sometimes more altruistic. However,
not all collaborative partnerships need be based on students who work well
together. There is much to learn when collaboration does not go smoothly,
as was the case when Emma and Serena collaborated. Classroom interactions involve endless negotiations. Listen to students' disagreements and
the strategies they use to try to resolve them. You may wish to use their negotiations as teaching tools by pointing out successful negotiations and
modeling ways to be an effective collaborator. Role-playing can be helpful
to teach students how to ask questions, ask for clarification, be persistent,
and take risks as they learn to collaborate. You may want to role-play examples of both successful and unsuccessful collaborations.

Sharing authority is another important element of collaboration
(Ruddell & Unrau, 1994). Many school tasks tend to focus on the

importance of knowing the right answer. It is important to let your students see that you are comfortable with not always having an answer, that you are able to share authority, and that you are willing to learn both with and from your students and varied other resources. This validates and confirms students' collaborative efforts as they see you sharing authority, too. Allow your students to see you asking questions and sharing information. You may want to share examples of collaboration from your own professional experience as well. Another way to further students' growth as collaborators is to involve them in Internet projects that reach outside the classroom, such as The Jason Project, at www.jasonproject.org, or Field Notes: Journey North Classroom Exchange, at www.learner.org/jnorth/l.

Creating an instructional climate that supports collaboration is a challenge. It involves small decisions, such as when to intervene in collaborative efforts, and larger decisions, such as when to allow students to solve problems on their own. It is important to teach students the strategies they will need to work with the Internet and various software programs, and it is equally important to teach the students how to work together effectively to share knowledge as they construct meaning. Collaboration involves creating a classroom climate where others' knowledge is valued. Increasing your own and your students' knowledge regarding the nature of effective collaboration is an important process that will enhance computer-based literacy activities in your classroom.

Reflection Point 4.6

1. If Ms. Coltrane had intervened in the students' collaborative efforts, what would have been gained? What would have been lost?

2. Collect further data on students' collaborative efforts in your classroom. Analyze and reflect on your data to gain an understanding of how collaborative efforts are successful and how they were not. What were the components of successful collaborations?

3. Have your beliefs about collaboration changed as you read and discussed this chapter? If so, how?

Jellyfish, Melodrama, and the Twilight Zone: Computer Explorations

Oliver and Joshua sit side by side at the classroom computer during literacy center time. Ms. Coltrane has asked them to experiment with the software The Magic School Bus Explores the Ocean *for their ocean research projects. On the screen, they see a bright yellow school bus poised to drop off a cliff into the midst of an underwater panorama. They begin to make predictions about what they are seeing.*

Oliver:	*Oh, it's like...where are we?*
Joshua:	*It's on an animal.*
Oliver:	*See that fish! [A bright blue and green fish and coral sea life flash on the screen.]*
Joshua:	*Is this a game? [Oliver and Joshua begin to experiment with the cursor and move to a different screen. They use the cursor to make the tide go up and down.]*
Narrated voice:	*The tide is low.*
[Oliver moves the arrow cursor again.]	
Joshua:	*Oh, Oliver! What is that?*

In Ms. Coltrane's classroom, students made use of the tool of technology in a variety of ways as they engaged in social and intellectual work to support their particular goals as meaning-makers. As they pursued specific goals, they were influenced by the interactive nature of computers. Computers, which may provide an abundance of multimedia, visual, semantic, syntactic, and phonic cues, can further literacy development as students are able to add to their knowledge of both how language works and what one can do with it.

As they used computers, students were exposed to elements of symbol systems that they were familiar with, such as letters, words, sounds, and pictures, and at the same time saw new forms of representation and new ways of making use of the familiar. For example, students discovered that they could incorporate images in their writing, listen to a reading of what they had written, and add musical elements to a story. Their explorations were characterized by a focus on experimentation, investigation, and discovery of the possibilities and potentialities of computers and what they could do with them. Salomon (1979) states that a medium is defined by how its symbol systems and technological attributes affect cognitive processing, and that a particular medium requires a learner to use a unique set of cognitive skills to derive meaning from that medium. For Ms. Coltrane's students, this need for and learning of a unique set of skills became evident.

As they explored with computers, Ms. Coltrane's students used a variety of meaning-making strategies. They had to figure out how to use the keyboard, move the mouse, move between pages, reverse directions with the cursor, use shortcut keys, move through different programs, understand graphics, and plan what they would do next. Some students were eager to explore, and others were hesitant to make mistakes. In this chapter, we will examine the different ways Ms. Coltrane's students responded to the invitation to explore with computers.

Seth: "I Couldn't Find Anything..."

When Seth sat down at the computer during literacy center time, he knew that he was supposed to conduct an Internet search for information that he could use in his individual ocean research project. The students in this class had been collecting ocean facts from books and computers in school and at home. Ms. Coltrane had shown the students how to use the search function at Yahooligans, a Web guide created for Yahoo that contains prescreened links.

Seth types in *freshwater jellyfish*, and clicks on the Search button. The search engine supplies him with a variety of matches, and he clicks on the *freshwater jellyfish* category at www.iup.edu/~tpeard/jellyfish.htmlx.

Oliver:　Now you're getting some facts.

Seth:　Yeah, this is good. [Seth clicks on "What do they look like?" and "Is there such a thing as a freshwater jellyfish?" He drags the cursor and scrolls down the page.]

Oliver:　They're flying in the darkness.

Seth:　Yahoo! Oliver, this is so fun! [As Seth begins to explore the different websites with increasing speed, he pays less and less attention to Oliver. He is moving so quickly that it is nearly impossible to read the words on the screen.]

Seth:　[as he clicks on pictures] I think it is searching, it's searching, it's searching.... [He flips the screen back and forth and up and down at dizzying speed. He clicks on an image to enlarge it.]

Oliver:　Oh, Seth, you got a whole bunch of facts!

Seth:　Oh, cool.

Oliver:　Better start looking.

Seth:　I hit the jackpot. I got, like, three paragraphs full of stuff in here. It seems like I have.... [Seth begins playing with the wrist gel pad instead of writing down any of the facts. He visits a large number of websites but spends only moments on each of them. He goes to the National Geographic site at www.nationalgeographic.com/world/9608/jellyfish/index.html and reads aloud.]

Seth:　"No bones, No brain. But what a sting." [He continues to read silently for a bit. At http://izzy.online.discovery.com/area/nature/jellyfish/jellyfish2.html, he clicks the mouse on a picture.] That's cool. My life as a blob. Oh, cool, Oliver, look at that jellyfish picture. [Seth stares intently at the screen and no longer comments to Oliver on what he finds.] Let's get up close on this one. Ooh, this is gonna be a great picture! Ooh! Ooh! [Seth follows a pattern of looking at a picture, clicking on it to get a larger image, viewing it, returning to the previous screen, and then repeating the process. At http://izzy.online.discovery.com/area/nature/jellyfish/survival.html, Seth watches a video about freshwater jelly-

> fish.] Ooh this is...look at this, doesn't it look like an alien
> ship? It looks sort of like an alien ship...I'm gonna try to do
> the whole.... [Seth continues to explore different websites.]

Rhett: Are you doing freshwater jellyfish?

Seth: Not really. I couldn't find anything.

Seth had, in fact, viewed an abundance of facts about freshwater jelly-fish in his explorations. Although he had seen many facts, he had col-lected none of them. His adventure was simply too engrossing to stop. Seth explored with bold, almost reckless abandon. He was amazed by what he saw and what he could do. Initially, Seth set out on a fact-finding mission. He was going to work on this activity with a friend. As he became more and more absorbed with what he was seeing and doing, however, his focus changed, and he became less conscious of his friend and more engrossed in what was in front of him rather than who was next to him. An abundance of images, sound, and motion drew in Seth. He was able to explore a vast repertoire of symbolic representations on his topic of fresh-water jellyfish. He was fascinated by the process of exploring as he clicked, scrolled, clicked again, downloaded, read, spoke, and moved at lightning speed. As Seth actively manipulated and navigated through a myriad of features, he read, reread, skimmed, and made choices about what he would investigate next. He was motivated by what he saw and what he could do, by what he could share and what he could keep his own. Seth did not accomplish the goal of gathering facts for his ocean research pro-ject, but he was immersed in a variety of active learning tasks and en-gaged in exploring varied representations of meaning.

At the end of the 90-minute literacy center period, Ms. Coltrane saw that Seth had not collected anything to use in his ocean research project. She knew that Seth was a quick-moving, energetic learner whose atten-tion she often needed to refocus on the task at hand. She decided that, at that moment, her long-term goal of having her students learn how to navigate the Internet was more important than her short-term goal of having them collect facts from Internet sources.

She also, however, knew that she wanted Seth to be more produc-tive. To encourage his productivity, she included him in the goal-setting process by asking him to make a reasonable judgment about how many facts he could collect in one 90-minute period and to use this number as his goal the following day. In this way, Ms. Coltrane gave Seth the freedom to explore in ways that he was comfortable with. Ms. Coltrane used what she knew about individual variation among students to decide how best to facilitate Seth's computer-based literacy learning. She modified her instructional goals as she saw how Seth went about constructing knowledge. Her teaching was responsive and fluid. Ms. Coltrane's instructional decision making was informed by her observation of how Seth used computers in the meaning-making process.

As Anderson-Inman, Horney, Chen, and Lewin (1994) suggest, not all students are ready to read and learn in hypertext environments, and each has a different style of using computers in literacy activities. Bikerts (1995) and Stoll (1995) express concern about students quickly and superficially exploring links rather than reading the information that is available on one link and processing it more deeply. Teachers need to be aware of each student's strengths and weaknesses as a learner and modify instructional decision making accordingly.

Reflection Point 5.1 _____

Seth's experiences illustrate the delicate balance between freedom and guidance that is continually renegotiated in responsive teaching and learning.

1. What factors do you think are important to consider when making decisions such as Ms. Coltrane's decision to focus on long-term goals?

2. One of the compelling features of browsing on the Internet is the ability to access hyperlinks that lead a user to new and different kinds of information. Brainstorm a list of strategies that you think would be helpful in achieving a balance between allowing students the freedom to explore and holding them accountable for the information they have found.

3. Discuss your ideas with a colleague.

Emma: Meeting the American Girls

Computers provide access to multisensory supports and opportunities to interactively manipulate and explore objects that may facilitate students' developing understandings of language (Carroll, 1999). The following example recounts Emma's explorations using the software program *The American Girls Premiere* (The Learning Company, 1999). The American Girls Premiere software is designed for children ages 8 to 12. It allows the user to write, direct, and produce a historical drama using the characters from the American Girls Collection series. Options include using varied backdrops (see Figure 6) and adding audio and music effects.

Emma goes to the Start menu on the classroom computer and scrolls through a list to find the software she is looking for. She explores varied im-

Figure 6
Screen From *The American Girls Premiere*

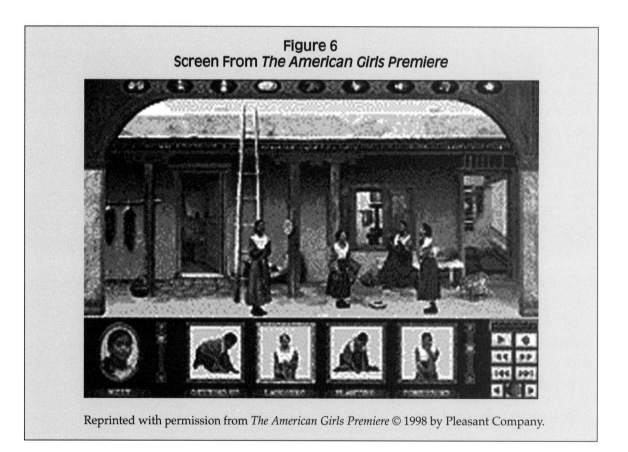

Reprinted with permission from *The American Girls Premiere* © 1998 by Pleasant Company.

ages and words that appear on the screen. As she moves the mouse over the bottom right-hand corner of the screen, the words Cue you can edit *appear. She clicks on* Characters, *and then on* Birthday. *Nothing happens. She clicks on* Characters *a second time and a character appears on the screen.*

Emma quickly realizes that changes occur when she moves the mouse, and she begins to experiment. She moves the character across the screen to a bed, and then in a circle.

Emma clicks on the word Music, *and several options representing the mood of the music appear. She chooses* Conflict. *Melodramatic music begins to play. She then chooses* Concern.

Emma then chooses the Text to speech *option. When a text box appears, she types* hihihi *and then erases it. A variety of props appear on the bottom of the screen when she chooses the* Props *button. She selects a prop, and then* Governor's Ball room, *and a new, detailed background appears.*

Emma was engaged in a rich multimedia experience where the fun was in the exploring. She manipulated the various elements on the screen as she explored what she could do and what the machine would allow her to do. The computer provided Emma with an enlarged repertoire of symbolic representations of meaning. Not only could she read her character's name but also she could move her across a screen, change the visual elements in the setting, experiment with different musical elements, type text, and use her own voice via a recording feature to become a part of the story. She had a rich and varied symbolic repertoire from which to choose.

Emma had to reflect on the differing forms of representation and make choices about how she would go about constructing meaning. For example, she saw meaning represented in certain symbolic forms such as words and images, and then she took action by making choices about what to do next within the context of the program. Her goal was to find out what she could do, and thus she experimented. She was motivated to continue her explorations by what she found and what she wanted to find out more about.

Ms. Coltrane allowed Emma the freedom to explore a software program in her own way. She did not direct Emma's explorations. This software program, by virtue of its open-ended design, was an excellent forum for Emma to explore varied symbolic elements of meaning.

Reflection Point 5.2

Knowing your own and your students' comfort levels with exploration is important. Surveys provide a chance to examine different aspects of exploration.

1. Fill out the teacher survey (see Figure 7) before giving your class the student survey (see Figure 8).

2. Reflect on your answers and your students' answers to the survey questions. Although these surveys are brief, they may help you to learn about individual variation in comfort levels with open-ended exploration. Some people are more comfortable with structure, and others find it constraining. This is especially important in school, where much of the instructional time is highly structured.

3. Select two students who seem to have different comfort levels with exploration, and observe them over the course of one week. What did you notice about their behaviors? Try to use what you have learned in planning your instructional goals.

Figure 7
Teacher Survey

Directions: Read each statement and place a check mark in the column that corresponds with your answer.

	Never	Often	Always
When I travel, I always use a map.			
When I read a chapter in a textbook, I preview chapter headings and the table of contents.			
When I read a book, I always read the foreword.			
When I have a plan, I usually follow it.			
I prefer to explore new places without a plan.			
My lesson plans usually work out the way I imagine.			

Figure 8
Student Survey

Directions: Read each statement and place a check mark in the column that corresponds with
       your answer.

	Never	Often	Always
When I go to a new place, I like to know what is going to happen before I get there.			
When I have friends over, we plan what we are going to do before they arrive.			
I like having nothing to do.			
I like reading about new things.			
I like it when my teacher tells us exactly what to do.			
I like knowing how a book is going to end.			
I like having a plan to do things in school.			

Both Seth and Emma found the freedom to explore exhilarating. They were motivated by what they saw on the screen and were eager to interact with the different graphics, words, and photographs they saw. Csikszentmihalyi (1990) argues that motivation to read is closely connected to opportunities to experience a sense of enjoyment while reading. Both Seth and Emma experienced this sense of enjoyment while reading on the computer during their explorations. Also, it is important to realize that knowledge is constructed through multiple perspectives as learners become aware that there are many ways to access information and to use language (Rose & Meyer, 1994).

Elena: No Match Found for Twilight Zone

Elena also was given the time and freedom to search the Internet, but her experiences were very different from those of Seth and Emma.

    Ms. Coltrane: I will be working with you on some search strategies.

    Oliver: We can use Yahooligans. [All four class computers are bookmarked for Yahooligans.]

Ms. Coltrane:	How do you know which links are going to be helpful?
Rhett:	You would click on the ones with whales.
Elena:	How you do this?
Serena:	Click on this. [Serena and Elena are sitting at adjacent computers. Serena points to a box.] Do your thing.

Ms. Coltrane comes back and asks the girls if they have some ideas. Elena types in *twilight zone* and gets the message *No match found for twilight zone.*

Elena:	I got nothing. Look, I didn't find anything. [Elena looks at Serena and Oliver.] I can't learn anything. It just says *twilight zone*. [Elena sees that the other students have more websites to search and she does not. Ms. Coltrane reads the words on Elena's screen.]
Ms. Coltrane:	Do you know what the words *No match found for twilight zone* mean?
Elena:	No.
Serena:	You can just go to *deep sea*.

Serena comes over to Elena's computer and moves the cursor into the prompt box. Elena types in the words *deep sea*. Elena begins to scroll down the page. She clicks on *animals* and accesses the link www.yahooligans.com/Science_and_Nature/Living_Things/Animals/Marine_Life/Fish/Viperfish/. Elena then clicks on the words *Marine Life* in the category bar at the top of the screen and accesses the page http://www.yahooligans.com/Science_and_Nature/Living_Things/Animals/Marine_Life/, which is a list of further links.

| **Elena:** | OK, this is better. Coral reefs would help. [Then she clicks on *dolphins* and arrives at www.yahooligans.com/Science_and_Nature/Living_Things/Animals/Mammals/Marine_Mammals/Dolphins, another list of links. Elena begins to scroll down the screen. Again, she compares what she is doing to what Serena is doing. She sees that Serena has different kinds of information on her screen, such as pictures and other graphics. Elena just has words and does |

not realize that once she has her initial search results, she has to click on one of them to move to a website with further information.] Where are you? How did you get there?

Serena: I searched different things. I'll get there for you. Go back down. Back to home page.

Elena: I'm looking at this. I do not know what to do on this. I look at this…. [Elena then decides to go back to the beginning. She hits the back button three times.] OK, here I was…I don't get what to do. [She scrolls down the page and looks at Serena and Oliver.] How you do this?

Serena: What are you trying to do?

Elena: I'm trying to find ocean animals.

Serena believes Elena is having a problem making a choice of which link to follow.

Serena: You've did *deep sea.* You pick the one you're interested in.

Elena then decides that it must be the words she is using to search that are causing her to have problems.

Elena: I'll just do *deep sea.*

Serena: You can do that by using the bar or the arrow. [Serena clicks in the box to set the cursor correctly, and then Elena types *ocean animals* and clicks on the next search option.]

Elena: Next search?

Serena: Yes, yes. [Elena hits *next search* and arrives at http://search.yahooligans.com/search/ligans?p=ocean+animals. Still, Elena does not seem to realize that she has to click again to move off the screen that simply lists the search results in words. She scrolls down the page. Elena decides to ask Serena again, but this time Serena does not give her any helpful information because she is not really aware of what the problem is.]

Elena: How should I find the...?

Serena: [believing there is a connection difficulty] It's a waiting thing. That always happens to me. It's a waiting thing—it always takes an hour.

Elena clicks on *Ocean Animals* and arrives at the site http://mbgnet.mobot.org/salt/animals/index.htm. She clicks on the words one more time and her search results begin to look like her classmates'. She then clicks on the words *common dolphin*. A picture appears on the screen. Elena finally realizes that she has to click on the search results to access a further link, but she doesn't know what to do with the information.

Elena: How you figure out? How would you do a project? I don't get it. You mean write down things, like, about an animal? You mean write down things about an animal?

Serena: Yes. [The girls are briefly distracted as they hold out their hands and compare their different nail polish colors.] It's the gold glitter against the blue glitter.

They laugh together, and then get back to work. Elena takes out her reading journal and writes *Ocean Project*.

Elena: How should, I should have just put *dolphins* in there. Uh, what do I write down? I forgot what I want my project to be about. Is yours about mazes? OK, Serena, never mind. Umm, Serena, what do we write down what our project would be about?

Serena: You just write down the site?

Elena: Should I write down *dolphins* since that is what my project would be about?

Serena: No, you write down the site. What did you type to get to that?

Elena: Should I write down *common dolphin*? I need to sharpen my pencil. [Under her title, Elena writes *common dolphin*.] Serena, is that all you have to write?

Literacy center time ends.

Elena needed to figure out what words meant in the new and unfamiliar context of an Internet search. Normally, she would simply read them to understand their meaning. She knew how to physically click on the mouse; what she did not know is that when she clicked on words, they would lead her to other websites. When she compared her results with those of her peers, she did not understand what she was doing incorrectly. This drove her to try other strategies, such as scrolling, but she was unsuccessful. After repeated efforts, she discovered that the words in this context represented links to further websites. Once she discovered how to use links, she had access to another symbolic representation of meaning. Frustration, motivation, and persistence defined Elena's experiences in using the Internet to search for information.

Although literacy center time ended before Elena was able to gather any information that she might have used in her ocean research report, she learned many important skills. She learned how to navigate through Internet links and how to experiment using a computer.

If Elena had been in a different instructional environment, her investigations might have followed a different path. She was given the time and the freedom to explore different aspects that technology afforded her, and ultimately she determined their meaning. Ms. Coltrane wanted her students to use the Internet as an information resource and learn Internet search strategies. Her goal was not to explicitly teach the strategies but for her students to learn to figure them out through exploration and experimentation.

One might argue that Elena wasted her time figuring out how to search. However, the abilities to tinker, monitor, adapt, guess, and adjust are critical to computer explorations. Elena was extremely persistent in her efforts to figure out how to do this assignment correctly. She was undaunted when she encountered difficulties. However, it is important to note that not all students will be as persistent as Elena. The key is to plan well for your students (see Box 5.1 for helpful resources, some of which include Internet lesson plans).

Box 5.1
Internet Resources

ArtsEdge Kennedy Center for the Performing Arts
http://artsedge.kennedy-center.org/content/2360
http://artsedge.kennedy-center.org/content/2358

The Global Schoolhouse
www.gsh.org

KQED Bay Area Mosaic Latino Heritage
www.kqed.org/w/mosaic/bumper.html

Maryland Public Television—Thinkport
www.thinkport.org

PBS Modern Dance and The Harlem Renaissance
www.pbs.org/wnet/freetodance/lessonplans_2.html

PBS National Geographic Africa
www.pbs.org/wnet/africa/tools/index.html

PBS Teacher Source
www.pbs.org/teachersource

Thirteen Ed Online, Mary Ann Patten: Clipper Ship Heroine
www.thirteen.org/edonline/lessons/clippers/index.html

Reflection Point 5.3

Internet exploring can be fruitful and frustrating. Leu and Leu (1999) state,

> Students left entirely on their own to surf the Internet will waste much time and learn little from their experiences. Students guided in their explorations of the Internet by a knowledgeable and thoughtful teacher will understand the world in new and powerful ways. (p. xi)

1. There are different opinions regarding Internet surfing, and many ways to use the Internet to help your students discover resources in literacy learning. You will need to reflect on how you want to best use the Internet to support your particular instructional goals.

What did you think of Elena's experiences?

What are your own experiences in surfing the Internet for information?

What guidelines would you use to make decisions on how much freedom to give your students as they explore the Internet?

2. Create a lesson that involves students exploring the Internet. (You may wish to use the Internet Scavenger Hunt on page 120). Evaluate the success of your efforts. What challenges did you encounter? What would you do differently in subsequent efforts?

Each student in Ms. Coltrane's class learned about the act of exploration from a different perspective as he or she used a computer to accomplish social and intellectual goals. Computers provided access to a variety of symbol systems and the opportunity to manipulate both the forms of language and the paths different explorations might take. As students explored, they were motivated to seek information about how different symbolic representations of meaning function. They could move words and objects, such as when Emma explored with *The American Girls Premiere* software; learn about jellyfish from varied perspectives and sources, as Seth did as he surfed the Internet; and implement varied strategies to obtain information, as Elena did in her efforts to search Yahooligans. Having access to multiple forms of symbolic representation can enhance students' reflection on the forms of language, which is a critical part of literacy development.

Reflection Point 5.4

1. In this age of increasing accountability and time pressures, how can you justify the time students spend exploring?

2. How can we find ways of using technology that incorporate students' voices, interests, and desire to explore within a highly structured literacy curriculum?

3. Why is exploration such a critical part of literacy development?

4. Discuss your answers with a colleague.

In Your Classroom

How can you use what you have learned about exploration in Ms. Coltrane's classroom to enhance literacy growth in your own classroom? The first challenge is to address the tension between exploration and accountability. The Internet contains vast amounts of information. It can be a helpful, but often overwhelming, research resource. As Kamil and Lane (1998) describe, being able to successfully use the Internet places special demands on the reader. Schmar-Dobler (2003) states that reading on the Internet demands students' abilities to activate prior knowledge, monitor and repair comprehension, determine important ideas, synthesize information, draw inferences, and ask questions. It is important to reflect on your students' learning experiences with computers so you can monitor their efforts as well as encourage their explorations.

It is also important to provide students with opportunities for self-directed explorations so they feel a sense of ownership when it comes to their learning. Assure students that it is not always necessary to have a predetermined path in learning. Computers offer a way to highlight multiple pathways and the open-ended nature of exploratory learning. The interactive nature of computers allows them to respond to individual needs in a supportive fashion (Hillinger, 1992; Leu & Reinking, 1996). As Dyson (1993) states,

> Young children from diverse backgrounds bring diverse experiences to symbol producing—talking, drawing, playing, storytelling, and, in our society, some kind of experience with print, all of which are resources with which both teachers and children can build new possibilities. (p. 6)

Different children use different forms of expression, have different understandings of the relations between letters and sounds, and use a variety of resources to solve problems. When we provide time for children to explore the capabilities and features of texts using computers, they gain information about how language works (Labbo, 1996).

It is important to encourage students to share the results of their computer explorations with others so they can learn from one another and see how valuable other students' knowledge can be. In Ms. Coltrane's class, the students eagerly shared with their peers what they found on the Internet and in varied software. This move can create a supportive and motivating atmosphere in which literacy exploration thrives.

Another challenge in students' computer explorations in literacy activities is the need to address students' comfort levels with risk-taking. Some students prefer more structured learning experiences, and others are quite adept at open-ended exploratory tasks. Optimal classroom conditions exist when students' approximations are valued and they are willing to try new ideas and behaviors (Ruddell, 1999).

Challenge students with exercises that stretch their comfort levels and their skills. Use what you know about individual learning styles to modify instruction. For example, for a student like Seth, structure can be a scaffold to learning. It is also important to think about your own comfort levels with exploration because when students explore, you have to be willing to accept that they may end up in different places than you might have planned for.

Resourcefulness and persistence are essential elements of computer use. You will encounter both hardware and software difficulties as you attempt to integrate computers into your classroom curriculum. Encourage your students to be active problem solvers and to share ideas and strategies among themselves. You may wish to create a problem–solution computer log that lists the problems students have encountered and their successes and failures in solving them. This can be a valuable class resource.

It is important to teach your students the value of exploration and let them know that you think it is a valuable part of learning. As Harste (1994) states, "It is when we are inquirers ourselves that we become the best teachers" (p. 1236). As you explore with computers in your classroom, there are many challenges but also many opportunities to enhance learning.

Chapter 6

Spiral Stairs and Musical Magic: Computer Play in the Classroom

Seth and Victor are using the word-processing software program The Amazing Writing Machine *(The Learning Company, 1996). The program is divided into five writing projects: Essay, Letter, Story, Poem, and Journal (see Figure 9). Each project offers templates for students to write text, import graphics, or create their own illustrations.*

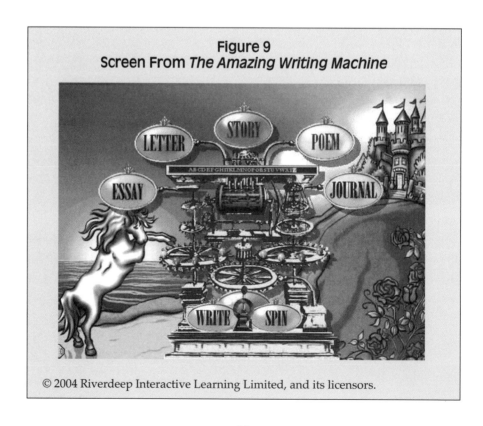

Figure 9
Screen From *The Amazing Writing Machine*

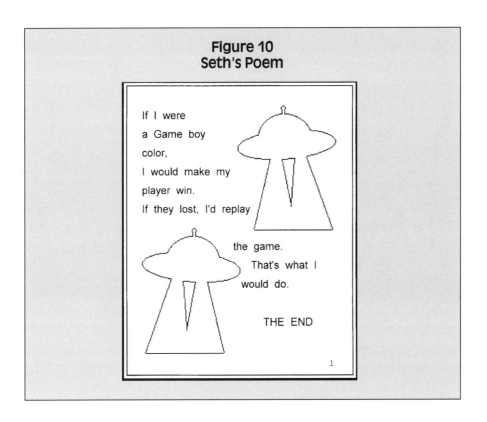

Figure 10
Seth's Poem

If I were
a Game boy
color,
I would make my
player win.
If they lost, I'd replay
the game.
That's what I
would do.

THE END

1

Rhett and Lily stand behind Seth and Victor as the boys tinker with
an astounding array of graphics. Seth changes the color of his sketch
lines until he decides on the final illustration to accompany his poem
(see Figure 10).

Seth: Oh, cool.
Victor: It looks like spiral stair.
Seth [singing]:   Waa-o-ay-ayayadiyadidyadiay.
Victor: I know, that's cool!
Seth: We-ing-wee-zoing, I'm doing everyone! Zweee!
                  [Seth moves his mouse up and across the screen.]
                  Wooo—let's do some slow. Woo! [He draws thicker
                  lines and he changes the color to a deep green.]
                  Knock-no-a-no-a-a-no.... [He sings out a new
                  rhythm as he continues to draw.] Oh, la, la, la, la,
                  la...I'm throwing all these spirals all over the place!
                  [As Seth drags a star across the screen, he hits the

Shift key.] BAM-BAM-BAM—no—we're going to
definitely have to radioactive this radioactive.
[Victor, Seth, Rhett, and Lily are enthralled as Seth
plays with his radioactive spirals.]

Seth: *That's a big layer of radioactive!*
Victor: *How did you make it huge?*
Seth: *I pressed the Shift key.*

Ms. Coltrane's students were playful: They played as they worked, they played at recess, and they played as they learned. They played as they read and as they wrote. And when given the opportunity to use a computer, they played with it as well. For example, as the vignette illustrates, Seth played with the different graphic options *The Amazing Writing Machine* program provided, and he invited his classmates to join his fun.

In this chapter, we will learn how Ms. Coltrane's students played with computers in a variety of ways. This playfulness was an integral part of how the students were discovering literacy and its role in their lives as learners. This was not a silent and controlled classroom but rather one that thrived on busy, joyful noise. The students in this class were comfortable being kids. They spilled things, knocked over chairs, and laughed often and easily. They imagined monsters in the pencil sharpeners and fiddled with erasers and lumps of clay. Play was part of who they were. In this classroom, the computer was a resource that was used to have fun. At times it fostered students' engagement in tasks and supported their learning, and at other times it was a distraction.

Reflection Point 6.1

Using computers can be a fun-filled experience. It is helpful to play with computers yourself as you think about how they can best support and enhance your literacy goals.

1. Choose a topic that is of interest to you but that you do not know a lot about. It need not be literacy related. Use a search

engine such as Yahoo (www.yahoo.com) or Google (www.google.com) to begin your search. Explore at least 15 Internet sites on the topic you have selected.

2. Choose three games to play from the choices at the Yahooligans games website at www.yahooligans.com/content/games.

3. What surprised you the most as you explored? What was the most fun part of your experience? What did you learn that you did not know?

Affective influences, such as motivation and engagement, are a critical part of children's play as they engage in socially constructed meaning-making. Children play with the forms of language and with one another as they develop as literacy learners. They experiment with the diversity of meanings in language through variation, association, and contrasts (Cazden, 1976). The importance of play in literacy development cannot be overlooked, as Bruner (1985) explains:

> I have never in all that time [of observing children's play] seen a child glaze over or drop out or otherwise turn off while engaged in play. I wish I could say the same for the children I have observed in classrooms and even in one-to-one tutorials. (p. 604)

Labbo (1996) describes how children's playfulness becomes apparent as they explore different elements of language with computers. Chang and Osguthorpe (1990) found that children were motivated and engaged when they worked with a picture–word processor program. Children enjoy using computers because they are a visual, exciting, and fun medium (Carroll, 1999).

Reflection Point 6.2

Play is an essential but often overlooked part of classroom learning. A playful atmosphere can be conducive to learning, but it also can be a detriment. A key factor is how the teacher views play. It is important to examine your comfort level with children's playfulness in your own classroom.

1. What are your thoughts regarding play among the students in your classroom? Do you feel it distracts or supports students' learning? List three examples of how play looks in your classroom.

2. Ask your students to discuss what they think about play and how it can help them learn. Their insights may surprise you.

3. Over the course of a week, take observation notes of students at work and play. As you review your data, examine how students' play affected their learning. Look for times when playfulness was a natural part of learning. After reflecting on your data, brainstorm a list of ways that you can use play to foster literacy learning. Keep track of how successful your ideas are.

Serena: "I Was Just Looking What It Would Sound Like"

Serena used *The Amazing Writing Machine* to type and illustrate a poem she had written. Serena was bold and creative in her play; for her, fun was integral to the learning process.

Serena leans her reading journal, which contains her poem, "If I Were an Angel," between the keyboard and the desk. She begins exploring the program options. First, she selects the *Goodies* feature on the *Edit* menu. This feature allows her to hear different sounds while she types. Serena selects *Drums* as her font to type by. She clicks on *Music* and then *hear it*. After a few moments of listening to the music, she makes a change. She tries the *Vocal* and *Western* options and continues to type.

"I like music the best because when you type really fast you can hear music," she says. She types a string of random letters, laughs, and says, "I was just looking what it would sound like." Serena, in fact, had made a "whole composition" from the singular sounds of random letters by using this function of the program. She is smiling and delighted with herself and her song.

Serena is not content with just hearing music. She begins to enthusi-astically explore a range of template options:"Should I do clouds or apples or, oh, the tree?"

She selects different options and looks at each for a moment before she moves to the next. On the screen, flowers, apples, planes, spaceships, and leaves appear and disappear quickly.

She settles on a template with two clouds and begins to type.

> If I were a holy
> angel I would give
> all my superb
> presents to my
> wonderful sister
> b

She erases the *b,* and continues typing.

> If I were a holy
> Angel
> I would
> make everyone
> give the best
> presents to
> each other

Serena rereads what she has written and clicks her mouse on *Infosaurus,* a feature that functions like a thesaurus. When the word *wonderful* appears on the screen, Serena chooses *okay,* and the word is then pasted in her poem in lieu of *best.* Serena's creativity is astounding as she plays with the different options available in the *Infosaurus* feature. She types a string of letters, chooses the *Find Rhyme* option, and then tries to pronounce the resulting nonsense word the function suggests. She laughs with glee and decides to pose a challenge by typing the entire alphabet. The message *No match was found* appears on the screen.

Serena was inventive and bold in her play. She completed the as-signed task of typing her poem during the allotted time; yet she also was able to play while she worked. She explored the multiple symbol sys-tems that *The Amazing Writing Machine* provided. She moved between sounds, words, and the kinesthetic action of typing. She was engaged in figuring out not only what do to but also how to do it. She was absorbed and focused as she worked and played, and highly motivated by the fun she was having. Serena did the intellectual work she was required to do and had great fun doing it because of the symbolic representations that were available to her to express meaning. The computer program allowed Serena not only to "looking what it would sound like" but also to "see" what she "meant" as a creator of poetry using a machine that opened both her eyes and her ears in new ways.

Reflection Point 6.3

Computers provide students with fun and exciting ways to learn about letters, sounds, words, images, and graphics. As Harste, Burke, and Woodward (1994) assert, the negotiation of meaning is a problem-solving strategy. The more students reflect on language, the further opportunities they have to learn about what language can do and what they can do with it.

1. What do you think Serena learned about language as she played with the different features of this software program?

2. If you had observed Serena, what would you have suggested as a follow-up activity to enhance her further literacy learning?

Elena and Lily: "Why Don't You Stay in the Air?"

During literacy center time, Elena and Lily diligently worked on the math software program *Math Blaster* (Davidson, 1997). They tried to figure out what was asked of them and how to make everything work correctly. When they were stuck, they persisted and tried a variety of strategies.

As they experiment with the keyboard controls, Elena and Lily realize that when they press the space bar and an arrow key at the same time, they turn the main character, a space alien, into a bungee jumper. Suddenly, fun is central to learning.

Elena: You can type your name and I'll type mine. You can type and...

Lily: Let me help.

Elena: How 'bout can I type...11 plus...what is it?

Lily: Nine, 10, 11, 12, 13, 14, 15...

Elena types in a number and hits *Enter*. At this point in the program, the user can hit the meteors by using the mouse to click on them.

Elena: Can I try? [The girls work in rhythm. Lily counts, and Elena types in the answer to the math problem.] We got a diamond! [The next section of the program appears on the screen (see Figure 11).] I don't know how. I don't know how to do this. OK, I never played this before.

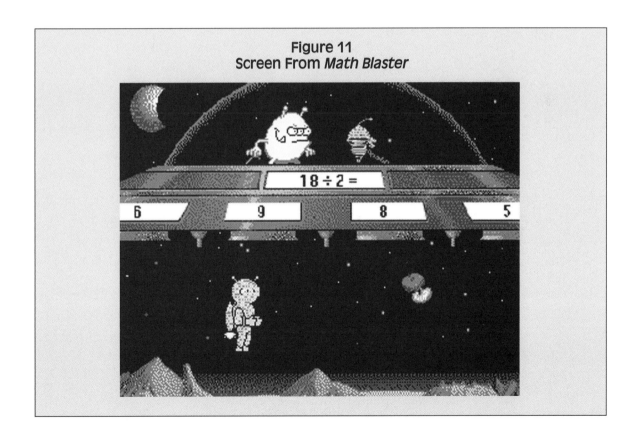

Figure 11
Screen From *Math Blaster*

Lily: Either have I. [Lily keeps the mouse.] You can play. [Lily puts Elena's hand on the mouse.]

Elena: Fifteen, 15, 14s, 15s. [Her voice gets louder and louder. Elena gives Lily back the mouse. She puts her hands over her mouth.] Go, Go! This is the hardest one. That's the one you have to get to.

Lily: It's a bungee jump. Come on! [Lily uses the cursor arrows to make the little space creature jump up on a block. Elena puts her hand over Lily's to press the keys.]

Elena: Oh, you try and get some diamonds. What do you do?

Lily: What do you do?

The girls have to figure out what to do next to move forward in the program because what they are doing is no longer working. Elena offers a few suggestions.

Elena: Go over there. [Lily hits the keyboard cursor arrows.] How about this one? You can't leave this one until you get to the top. You go over here. [She pushes the cursor arrow that moves the space creature to the right. Lily pushes her hand off. They both have puzzled looks on their faces.] You've got to get him to stay in the air.

The girls look at each other. Lily clicks on the *Help* function and the help screen appears. They leave this screen after only a few seconds, almost too quickly to have read much at all. As she hits the space bar and the arrow key at the same time, Lily makes a wonderful discovery.

Lily: I don't know what they mean. Oh, cool, I'm jumping!

Elena: Just jump all the time!

Lily: I'll stay in the air. I can stay in the air. Jump! Jump!

Elena: Why don't you stay in the air?

After this interlude ends, the girls get serious once again and return to work. They realize that they are unable to move anywhere else in the program.

Lily: I don't get this.

Elena: I don't get this either.

Lily   [looking over at Serena who was sitting at the computer next to theirs]: Do you know how to get out of this?

Serena: You got to do this.

Elena: We don't get it.

Serena: The number you get in your brain has to be between this and this. [She points to a blank space in the screen between two equations.]

Elena: OK, now what do we do when we have it in our heads?

Serena: Press *Enter*.

Elena: Keep walking that way.

Lily: Can't go that way.

Elena: Let me try it.

Lily: How do you get up?

Serena: You jump.

Elena: Oh...she got the character to jump by hitting the Ctrl key.

Lily: Hey, Serena, I'm stuck.

Serena: No, you're not jumping over there. [When they took Serena's advice, it made the little space alien jump in the air, and they dissolved with laughter once again.]

Lily: Jump! [She presses the Ctrl key.]

Elena: Don't jump on him or he'll kill you.

Lily: He'll jump on me!

Elena: Wait—don't press it at all. See if they'll tackle him—it's cool.

Elena and Lily were clearly enjoying working together on the program. They raised their voices in glee, frequently had smiles on their faces, and laughed loudly and often. They enjoyed what they were doing and the fact that they were doing it together. When they began the game, they were unsure about how they might "get some diamonds" by doing some math. As they tried to get the character to "walk," they were motivated to figure out how to "do" the math and "do" the game. The computer program provided varied symbol systems, such as numbers, images, and words, and the opportunity to manipulate them in different ways. The fun that the girls were having motivated them to continue to explore the math problems, and the program was designed so that they would continue doing more of the math as it built on skill sequences. Elena and Lily could have, however, made the choice to simply "stay in the air" for the rest of the game and never do another math problem. They did not. Instead, they chose to move forward. As illustrated in this example, children make choices about how to use the opportunities computers provide in different ways.

Reflection Point 6.4

It is important to look closely at the materials students play with as they learn about varied symbol systems by using varied computer software programs.

1. What motivated the girls as they used this computer program?

2. What role did the varied symbol systems (words, graphics, numbers, etc.) play in the girls' motivation?

3. If you had observed Elena and Lily, what would you have suggested as a follow-up activity to further enhance their learning?

It is important to closely examine the kinds of programs and Internet sites that students use. You need to set clear instructional goals and monitor how students are progressing. It is sometimes easy to assume that learning is occurring. In the following section, we see that this is not always true.

Brycen and Jamal: "Yeah—Got Some Nasty Right in the Face! Let's Keep Going to the Slime Place..."

Brycen and Jamal were working on the classroom computer using *Reading Blaster* (Davidson, 1997). According to the publisher, the purpose of this software is to improve student vocabulary. In the presentation activity, users are shown a word, its definition, and then a sentence using the word. Then, users are given a list of games to choose from. The boys de-

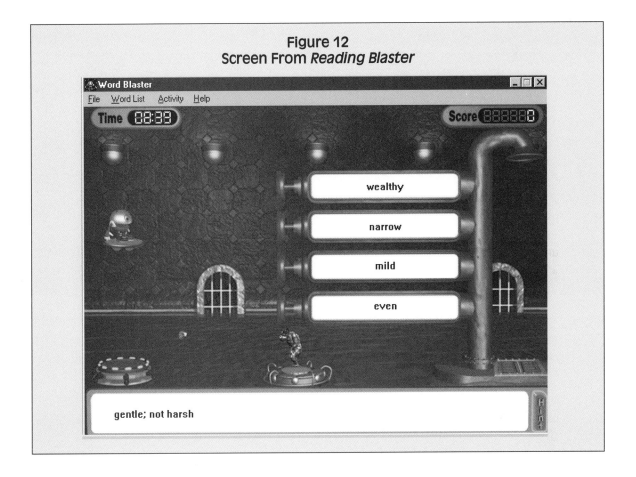

Figure 12
Screen From *Reading Blaster*

cided to play The Slime Game. In this game, users have to avoid the slime by deftly maneuvering characters by using both the mouse and keyboard while matching words with their definitions. Users have to hit the cursor arrow to position fireballs next to the word that matches the definition at the bottom of the page and use the space bar to shoot a fireball into the tube above the correct word (see Figure 12).

Brycen: Oh, here it goes. [Brycen clicks on the *Play* option.] Enter your name.

Jamal: Oh, I love that game!

A box at the bottom of the screen contains a definition: *living or being alone.* The boys begin to play.

Brycen: Fire. What if we get hit by the guy?

Jamal:	You don't get hit by the guy.

As they played, they moved the arrow next to the first word on the list and hit the space bar to shoot a ball into the tube. They proceeded down the list and did this to each of the word choices on the screen. They did not look for the synonym by reading; instead, they eventually found it by the process of elimination. After about seven minutes, they were finished.

Brycen sees their score of 2,500.

Brycen:	Oh.
Jamal:	We won, I think.
Brycen:	Let's go medium. What if we get hit? I want him to get me. Fire!

When he got slimed Brycen happily exclaimed, "Ooooh! Fire now you!"

In the more difficult level of the game, the object is to move the character up and down rapidly to avoid the slime at the same time as choosing a synonym for a given word. The boys move rapidly through the word choices.

Brycen:	Shoot me! Oooh, it keeps missing me! Come on, Yeah! Oh, I missed that one I was right on the.... Yeah—got some nasty right in the face! Let's keep going to the slime place. This time let's do it hard! As hard as you can...missed me. You gotta get me, come on you slow poke, skateboard, I'm coming down! I like him getting me, come and get me!
Jamal:	Now come and get me.
Brycen:	Hit me, hey, hey.
Brycen and Jamal:	Uhhh!
Brycen:	I'm on a flying skateboard, we'll—I'm not too good at driving these things. Oh, man, that thing was right for me. I don't know how to drive these flying skateboard things!
Teacher's aide:	Did you know there is a definition there? [She tries to tell them that the object of the game is to

	read the definition first in order to line up your character with the correct synonym.]
Brycen:	No, we're just trying each one. We were just running all of them. [Even after she tells them how to "correctly" play the game, they continue doing exactly what they had been doing.] Anyway. We got him.

The boys were highly motivated to play *Reading Blaster* because it was fun. This game may have been designed to encourage the student to focus on the vocabulary, yet in this case, the vocabulary learning was not tied to the fun. Ms. Coltrane's instructional purpose was to foster word learning, but Brycen and Jamal wanted to play a video game and had no interest in the vocabulary. They just wanted to have fun together.

In The Slime Game, the boys had an opportunity to explore different aspects of language, embedded in a visual, animated, and sound-filled environment. Because the game was fun and engaging, it would seem to have been a good choice to support word learning. However, Brycen and Jamal discovered that they could ignore the vocabulary and still "play" the game by evading slime and shooting accurate fireballs.

This example highlights the fact that students may not always take advantage of the opportunities that technology provides to enhance their literacy learning. Consequently, it is important to ensure that your students are using such computer programs appropriately.

*Reflection Point 6.5*_____

It is important to observe students' interactions as they are playing learning games on the computer to ensure that students' actions support your instructional goals.

1. What motivated Brycen and Jamal as they used this computer program?

2. What role did the varied symbol systems (words, graphics, numbers, etc.) play in the boys' motivation?

3. If you had observed Brycen and Jamal, how would you have intervened?

In Your Classroom

How can you use what you have learned about play in Ms. Coltrane's classroom to enhance literacy growth in your own classroom? First, it is important to provide your students with both opportunities and materials that will ignite their creativity and stimulate their playfulness. Activating children's motivation and interest is an important role for teachers (Gambrell, 1996), and play is a central component of literacy learning. The essence of play is the creation of imaginary situations (Franklin, 1983; Vygotsky, 1934/1978). Books, dramatic play, storytelling, music, and art have been used to enhance playful classroom literacy learning. What can computers add to this rich mix? As students use computers, they can hear a broad array of music, explore animations, conduct experiments, visit online museum exhibits, or talk with explorers (see Boxes 6.1 and 6.2 for

---

Box 6.1
Fun Websites to Explore

Amusement Park Physics
www.learner.org/exhibits/parkphysics

Girls, Inc.
www.girlsinc.org/gc/page.php?id=1.1.3

Museum of Web Art
www.mowa.org/home.html

PathFinder Science
http://pathfinderscience.net

PBS Jazz Kids
www.pbs.org/jazz/kids

San Francisco Symphony Kids Site
www.sfskids.org

Box 6.2
Miss Rumphius Award Winners

The Miss Rumphius Award is presented by members of the RTEACHER listserv, a listserv sponsored by the International Reading Association, to educators who develop and share exceptional Internet resources for literacy and learning (www.reading.org/awards/rumphius_comprehen.html).

Book Rap
http://rite.ed.qut.edu.au/oz-teachernet/projects/book-rap

Cinderella Around the World
www.northcanton.sparcc.org/~ptk1nc/cinderella

Earth Day Groceries Project
www.earthdaybags.org

Read a Book–Write a Poem: An Internet Project for First Graders
www.mrsmcgowan.com/winterpoems/index.html

Vietnam: A Children's Guide
www2.lhric.org/pocantico/vietnam/vietnam.htm

---

website resources). Students also can use word-processing programs that allow them to play with different shapes, graphics, words, audio, video, images, and forms as they read and write.

Another important element of incorporating play and literacy learning is to encourage students to play with each other on the computer. Daiute (1989) describes the experience of jointly exploring and playfully manipulating language in writing activities. This playfulness can be enhanced by using a computer. As you plan your instruction, look for opportunities for children to playfully explore language together.

You also should encourage individual, reflective kinds of computer play in your classroom. When students play alone, as Emma did, it often provides a more focused and thoughtful learning experience, and various studies have shown that children's responses are deeper and richer in an environment where their "wonderings" are encouraged (Raphael & McMahon, 1994; Silva & Delgado-Larocco, 1993). Individual play also provides students with opportunities to manipulate language and reflect on the forms of language. For some students, this can be a chance to privately practice reading, revisit unfamiliar words, listen to repeated readings of a story, or explore context clues in an unhurried manner. Talking picture books are an excellent resource for individual play because students can read and learn at their own pace.

Because there are so many different software programs available, you can begin comparing and evaluating software using the Superkids Educational Software Review at www.superkids.com. You also can hear stories at Kids Corner at http://wiredforbooks.org/kids.htm or the Storybook Online Network at www.storybookonline.net/Default.aspx.

It is important to monitor play, as became evident in Brycen and Jamal's experiences. We cannot and should not assume that children are using computer materials in optimal ways. As with all socially based learning activities, the fun can be a distraction to learning. You need to be aware of what is happening as students play and make individual decisions on when to intervene.

Last, it is important to celebrate play. Play is an essential and wonderful part of childhood. Focusing on the role of play can enrich our own lives as educators. Dyson (1989) describes how it is important to engage in playful talk with children because it makes us aware of the happy mix of childhood and language. Dyson (1989) states,

> It is easy to pull written language out of the constellation of symbol systems of which it is a part and within which children experience it. Moreover, it is easy to treat that written language as a subject for the child to learn in school, rather than as a tool for the child's playful and thoughtful expression. (p. 271)

Computers in the classroom remind us that play is a critical part of literacy learning. You can learn a lot about children's literacy growth and enhance the quality of your instruction by observing and participating in children's playful activities.

"It's Always OK to Ask a Buddy": Challenges and Opportunities in Technology Integration

Elena, Seth, Analia, Serena, Emma, and Joshua are sitting at a round table tucked in a cozy corner of the classroom. They are listening to Ms. Coltrane explain the literacy center activity they will be doing on the classroom computers.

Ms. Coltrane: *I'm going to have you do some exploration of an ocean website. I want you to start reading for information. If you need help, it's always OK to ask a buddy. Here are the steps to follow. [Ms. Coltrane points to the whiteboard behind her on which she has written the steps.]*

You need your reading journal.

1. Open bookmark: Science Learning Network

2. Click on *Explore Resource*

3. Click on *Ocean's Alive*

4. Browse and read different links for 10–15 minutes

5. In your reading journal, record

    3 interesting oceanography facts that you've discovered

    2 possible project ideas

    2–5 unanswered ?'s you have that your reading made you think of

The students pair up and excitedly begin the activity.

Analia: *Emma, do you want to type?*

Emma: *No, you do it. I'll do the mouse. I can't type.*

Ms. Coltrane prepared her students, integrated the computer activity with classroom literacy practices with which the students were familiar, encouraged collaboration, and gave clear directions to follow. She included open-ended and structured components in the activity, and she trusted her students to use each other as resources. Teachers play a critical role in implementing effective instructional activities in the literacy curriculum.

The Future of Technology Integration

Throughout the book, Ms. Coltrane and her class have provided a glimpse of the multiple possibilities for meaning-making that technology introduces into literacy instruction. We have seen challenges, struggles, and successes. We have seen how students collaborated, explored, and played with computers to achieve both social and intellectual goals. And most important, we have seen the challenges and tensions that teachers face in using technology to enhance literacy learning.

Today, new literacies emerge as new information and communication technologies demand new skills for their effective use (Leu & Kinzer, 2000; Leu, Mallette, & Karchmer, 2001; Luke, 2000; Reinking, McKenna, Labbo, & Kieffer, 1998). Selfe (as cited in Pianfetti, 2001) describes how "the definition of literacy has expanded from traditional notions of reading and writing to include the ability to learn, comprehend, and interact with technology in a meaningful way" (p. 256). It is important to keep learning about these changes and think about the effect they have on your students. As Leu (2000) states, the new literacies are continually changing and will continue to challenge our definitions of what it means to be literate. Dalton and Grisham (2002) describe the importance of infusing literacy curricula with technology in meaningful ways and harnessing the power of technology to not only support traditional literacies but also the new literacies connected with the Internet and other forms of digital communication. Our students face many challenges as computers become an increasingly important element in everyday life experiences. Proficiency in the new literacies of the Internet—Internet browsers, e-mail, instant messaging—will become essential to our students' literacy future (International Reading Association, 2002), and students also will need to know how to use word processors, CD-ROMs, DVDs, and presentation software.

Another important aspect of technology integration involves looking closely at the specific attributes of technology and how they affect literacy learning. Kinzer and Leu (1997) describe how the complexity available to the computer user in terms of graphics, traditional text, sound, video, and animation calls for an increase in the user's strategic knowledge and affects his or her reading and writing. Labbo and Kuhn (1998) describe how word-processing programs allow the writer to view the emerging text as malleable. With word-processing programs, there is no longer an expectation that students must move through the stages of the writing process sequentially. As students write using computers, they must accommodate the ways in which the writing process is affected by technology (Baker & Kinzer, 1998). An awareness of how the computer affects the writing process is a critical aspect of your instructional planning.

The reading process outside word processing also is affected by the new potentialities computers introduce. Reading in hypertext is a challenge for students (Reinking, 1997), as evidenced by Elena's Internet explorations. Many websites present pages in nonlinear fashion, inviting readers to chart their own course through the text, images, audio, and video information. Anderson-Inman, Horney, Chen, and Lewin (1994) found that some students may not be ready to read and learn in hypertext environments. This kind of reading, they argue, requires development of traditional reading skills, computer skills, and special skills to navigate and read hypertext. Sutherland-Smith (2002) reports that students "perceive Web text reading as different from print text reading" (p. 664). Students may find that without the linear format they find in traditional print, they are unable to follow the author's message and make sense of what they are reading. This is particularly important with novice readers who may have more difficulty maintaining a coherent sense of meaning in a complex hypertext environment. Creating effective instructional scaffolds and strategies for hypertext is a critical element of your literacy curriculum.

Students' multimedia presentations also are shaped by the capabilities of the tools they are using. For example, students can combine text, pictures, images, and sound to create presentations. They can add sound effects, record their own stories, import video clips, and add music as they create their own stories. In hypertext learning environments, students are able to combine various symbol systems in multilinear formats

(Grisham, 2001). The use of varied multimedia tools can support experimentation with the forms of language. It is important to be aware of how varied media shape students' growing literacy understandings.

Teacher education programs are grappling with how to best prepare new teachers to integrate technology into the curriculum (Mallette, Karchmer, & Leu, 2001). (See Figure 13 for some recommendations on how to effectively integrate technology.) School administrators are challenged by budgetary and policy constraints in the use of technology. Schools, communities, legislators, educational researchers, activists, and politicians are working to address the digital divide, where some schools and communities have access to a multitude of computer resources while others have few or none. Technology challenges us to ask new questions regarding our beliefs and assumptions about the teaching–learning process that affect students' lives both in and out of the classroom.

Throughout this book, I have described how technology was integrated into one class's literacy curriculum. As we shared the stories of Ms. Coltrane and her students we were able to reflect on the nature of classroom interactions around computers and gain insights into the complex nature of the teaching–learning process. We saw how the specific attributes that technology offered affected students' discoveries about the potential and possibilities of language.

Figure 13
Effectively Integrating Technology Into the Literacy Curriculum

1. Be willing to take risks and experiment with computers.

2. Provide time and support for learners to make both mistakes and discoveries as they use computers.

3. Model effective reading and writing strategies for students as they use computers in literacy activities.

4. Encourage students to collaborate as they use computers.

5. Validate students' needs to explore without a preset destination in both computer-based and non–computer-based literacy activities.

6. Celebrate playfulness while using computers in classroom literacy activities.

What can we conclude from this study about how to best use computers in an elementary classroom? First, it is important to realize that computers are tools for meaning-making that are embedded within existing classroom cultures. Computer use cannot and should not stand alone. It must be integrated into the literacy curriculum, not added to it.

Second, Ms. Coltrane's students used the classroom computers in a variety of ways as they engaged in social and intellectual work to support their particular goals as meaning-makers. They had easy access to multiple forms of symbolic expression and were able to construct knowledge from multiple perspectives. These varied symbol systems provide an enlarged repertoire that they were able to use to gain information about how written language works.

Third, students used computers within social relationships. Students' literacy learning is influenced by their social relationships with one another, the expectations and instructional goals of their teacher, the task at hand, the roles they take on, and the varied components of the tools they use to construct meaning.

Teachers must reflect on how they want to use computers to support their instructional goals. There is no one best way to incorporate technology into the classroom for all learners because computer use is about discovery. Its function should not be to replace the established instruction, but to enhance it. The best that educators can do is closely observe how children learn and make decisions to determine how to best support their instructional goals for literacy development.

Reflection Point 7.1 _____

As you read the stories of Ms. Coltrane's classroom, you saw the challenges of one teacher's journey to integrate technology into the literacy curriculum.

1. Revisit some of your earlier reflections and writing. How have your beliefs about literacy and technology changed as you read this book?

2. What change surprised you the most?

3. Create a visual map by using images and text to show your journey. Share your map with a colleague.

In Your Classroom

The relationship between technology and literacy is complicated, and many questions remain. How can you use the insights you have learned from Ms. Coltrane's classroom in your own classroom?

First, we have seen how important it is to focus on the nature of students' social interactions. Computer use invites more collaborative activities, and the skill of effective collaboration is highly valued both inside and outside school. You can use what you observe about how children interact to create productive literacy collaborations.

We also have seen the importance of encouraging students to explore the vast resources of the Internet and the inviting array of software programs that are available. Again, you need to use your insights about individual students to build effective literacy practices that invite them to explore. Explicit instruction in these areas can help your students to grow as literacy learners. Being a model for students in risk-taking, problem solving, and using others as resources is critically important. Be willing to create a class webpage with your students, to explore a new Internet site, to search for answers to a science problem on the Internet, or to try a new interactive game. Your willingness to explore with technology sends a powerful message to your students about how important it is to take risks in learning. As Leu (2002) states, learning to learn is at the core of the new literacies.

Play has always seemed a difficult area to discuss in relation to literacy. By its nature it evokes frivolousness. Yet to ignore play is to ignore a vital component of children's lives. I have always found that children's conversations and ways of looking at the world offer an amazing and insightful perspective on learning. Playing with computers with your students allows you to see a glimpse of their personalities you may not often see in school. I believe that if we truly listen to children's voices we will learn more about literacy than can ever be learned from a text.

Reflection Point 7.2_____

Ms. Coltrane struggled with the challenges of integrating technology into the literacy curriculum.

1. What will be your greatest challenge as you integrate technology into your literacy curriculum?

2. How would you describe your instructional goals related to technology? If you had to choose one aspect of technology as the most important for students to learn, what would you select?

3. What area of technology-related literacy is of greatest interest to you? Set specific goals to help you pursue your interest.

4. How will you use the insights you have gained from this book to become a more reflective practitioner?

Conclusion

This study was, as Geertz (1973) describes, "not an experimental science in search of law, but an interpretive one is search of meaning" (p. 34). I learned much from my time with Ms. Coltrane and her students. As we integrate technology into our classroom lives, we cannot overlook the power of using others as learning resources. As Leu (2000) states,

> The connectivity that characterizes literacy on the Internet permits all of us to learn from one another in ways never before possible. As a result, the more members of the literacy community that enter these worlds, the more insights we can bring to central issues of instructional practice. Even if you are just getting started, you have important information to share with others—questions that get everyone thinking critically about how to best use the new technologies of literacy. In a connected world, good questions are often the most useful information because they prompt thoughtful answers from which others may also benefit. (p. 427)

My hope is that the story of Ms. Coltrane's classroom has inspired you to reflect on your own practice as you integrate technology into the literacy curriculum. Let the insights you have gained help you to imagine new possibilities, ask endless questions, delve into unknown adventures, and—with your students—turn cartwheels on the classroom keyboard.

Classroom Data Analysis

Themes

There were three main themes that became evident in my data analysis: collaboration, exploration, and play.

Collaboration

I developed this theme by focusing on evidence in the data that was characterized by a focus on shared action. Issues of negotiating power, status, and control of the direction of the event are forefronted. Collaboration may look like an equitable partnership, a collision of differences, or dynamic ongoing shifts on a continuum of support–control throughout the event. Collaboration requires the ability to monitor one's own learning and a peer's learning, communicate one's needs effectively, and assess the ongoing pursuit of a specific goal within the interaction.

Exploration

I developed this theme by focusing on evidence in the data that was characterized by a focus on experimentation, investigation, and discovery of the possibilities and potentialities of computers and/or what one can do with them.

Play

I developed this theme by focusing on evidence in the data of students' sense of enjoyment and pleasure, and the idea that a computer is a resource that can be used to have fun.

Student Purpose

The student purpose within the computer-based literacy event was defined as relational or task based. The relational aspect was characterized by an interaction. The task-based aspect was characterized by an action specific to pursuing a goal.

Examples of Relational Purposes include the following:

1. Negotiating power

   A child is in control of the mouse while working on a software program. She is able to vary the shade of a character's skin color and asks another child's opinion: "I like that. She's brown lady. Do you like that [other color] or do you like brown?"

2. Soliciting help from a peer

   Two children are working together on an Internet activity and one child says to the other, "I can't read this—what am I supposed to do?"

3. Cooperating effectively with a peer

   Two children are reading information on a website. One child is reading aloud and asks the other, "Do you want to read now?"

4. Working on an activity with a peer

   Two children sit next to each other at adjacent computers. They are working on the same activity, looking for facts to use in their research project. One child says, "Oh, Oliver, you got a whole bunch of facts!" and the other answers, "Oh, cool."

5. Inviting a peer to share a software program

   One child begins to explore a CD-ROM that is based on a series of dolls and books that she is familiar with. She says, "Emma, are you sure you don't want to play?"

6. Sharing work and having fun with a peer while using a software program

   Two students are playing a math game in a software program. They move one of the characters by hitting the arrow cursor, and it looks like the character is jumping into the air. One child says to the other with a big smile, "Just jump all the time!"

7. Soliciting attention for products and/or actions

A child is using a word-processing program to type and publish her poem. She turns around in her seat and asks an adult helper, "Should I do clouds?" when choosing a template and says, "I like the music best because when you type really fast you can hear music," while choosing a musical typing font.

8. Having fun while playing a software game with a peer

Two children are sitting next to each other at the computer. One child says excitedly to his peer, "Let's leave this activity—it's really weird. Let's go medium. What if we get hit? I want him to get me. Fire! Ooooh! Ah-ooh—he missed me! Fire now you!"

9. Sharing discoveries with a peer

While using a word-processing program, one child makes a swarm of sound effects as he draws a picture by using the mouse. He says to his friend, "Look at this Victor.... WWWWOO-W-ZZZZZ-ZZZZZ-ZZZZZZZZZRRHRRRRR. Ow-wee-oo-wo-wo-e-wo. Splendi-dee!"

Examples of task-based purposes include the following:

1. Investigating a software program

In a computer program, the student manipulates underwater diving gear to swim around and explore plants, fish, mammals, crustaceans, and other creatures in the sea. One child says to a peer, "We're going down deeper. Is this where a trench is?" The child is focused on finding out what constitutes the software program and what can be done within the context.

2. Typing a poem using a software program

The child is using a word-processing program to type a poem she first wrote by hand. The child is focused on finding out what she can do using the components of the program as she completes the typing task. The child used the *Goodies* feature on the *Edit* menu, and then chose the *Music* option. This gave her a variety of musical options that would play as she typed. She chose *Drums* as her font to type by.

3. Conducting an Internet search for facts to use in a research project

Two children working on adjacent computers both typed in the letters that would bring them to the www.yahooligans.com website, where they began their search for facts about their ocean-related topics. One child typed in *freshwater jellyfish* and clicked on the *Search* button. He came up with the site matches and clicked on the category *freshwater jellyfish* at www.iup.edu/~tpeard/jellyfish.htmlx.

4. Investigating how the Internet functions

Two children are working at adjacent computers. One child says to the other, "Where are you? How did you get there?" The other child answers, "I searched different things. I'll get there for you. Go back down. Back to *home page*." The first child says, "I'm looking at this. I do not know what to do on this. I look at this." She decides to go back to where she began. She hits the *back* button three times. "OK here I was...." She scrolls back and says, "I don't get what to do."

5. Determining how a software program game works

Two children are working at a computer together as they try to figure out how to play a game. "Go over there," suggests one child. The other one responds by pushing the keyboard arrows harder. The first child says, "How about this one? You can't leave this one until you get to the top. You go over here," and she pushes the cursor arrow that moves a space creature on the screen to the right. The other child pushes her hand off. They both have puzzled looks on their faces. The first child says, "You've got to get him to stay in the air."

6. Typing a poem together using a software program

Two children sit together at one computer. One child is typing the other child's essay for him. "Do you need flying cars that make you go really fast?" she asks the author. "Comma, comma and... here, do you want to get that out of there?" She refers to the rectangular box for graphics in the middle of the text page. She clicks on it and erases the box.

7. Investigating a website

Two children are working together at one computer. They are exploring different sections of a website. One child says, "Where are the fun and games?" They click the mouse on a section of the website. The other child says, "Go down there. Go back there—this, let's go to one of those." The first child says, "No, let's go to Hogwarts and Harry."

Roles

Students took on the following roles within the computer-based literacy event:

1. Controller: One who usurps power and takes charge

   Two children are working together at one computer. One is typing. She erases an entire paragraph of text. The other child says, "What the heck are you doing?" The first child answers "We're doing it over. We're doing it over."

2. Supporter: One who encourages other's efforts

   Two students are playing a game using a computer program. The object is to win a 'Fish Card' before your turn ends. As the first student begins his quest in a new game, the second student says, "Oh gosh, Nick, I'm all wah, wah (mimicking tears)! She didn't eat us? Goooooooo!!"

3. Seeker: One who solicits assistance

   Two students are working together on an Internet activity. The first child says to the other child, "I can't read it."

4. Persister: One who perseveres

   Two students are working at adjacent computers. They are searching the Internet for facts that they will use to write their individual research projects. The first student is confused and continues throughout the event to try to figure out how to do this task by doing different things and by asking questions. At one point she asks the other student, "Where are you? How did you get there?" Then later she says, "I don't get what to do." At a later point she says, "How you figure out? How would you do a project? I don't get it. You mean write down things like about an animal? You mean write down things about an animal?" The second student answers, "Yes."

5. Student: One who has an interest in getting an assigned task done

   Two students are working together at one computer using a computer-based math game. The numerical problem 11 + 5 appears on the screen. The first child slowly types the answer, and the second child hits *Enter*. The first child says, "My turn, OK, the next time I get to. Oh, big ones, lucky." They work in rhythm and then switch tasks. The first child then counts and types in the answer, and one of them hits *Enter* depending on how long the other is taking.

6. Creator: One who innovates, using the computer for aesthetic purposes
One child works alone at the computer. She is typing her poem using a word-processing program. One of the options available is to hear music as one types. She types in a random string of letters and says, "I was just looking what it would sound like."

7. Buddy: One who is focused on shared social relations
For example, two children are investigating a website and creating questions that they could ask the author of a book. The first one says, "Let's answer the questions. Let me see what I would ask her—I would ask her...." The second child interrupts and suggests, "Can you make video games?" The first child then says, "Can I have your big giant humongo eye glass?" and they dissolve in laughter.

8. Mentor: One who is focused on supporting the efforts of a peer through monitoring, questioning, assessing, and helping
Two children are working together as they read an Internet site and answer questions. The student who is the more capable reader says to the other child, "Are you listening?" "You already wrote it, why did you scratch it out?" and "Do you get it?" She points out where she is reading from, using her finger to touch the screen.

9. Game Player: One whose primary focus is on the arcade-like qualities of a computer program
Two students are playing a computer-based game about words and their definitions. The first student says, "Yeah—got some nasty right in the face! Let's keep going to the slime place. This time let's do it hard! As hard as you can [unclear]... missed me. You gotta get me, come on you slow poke, skateboard, I'm coming down! I like him getting me, come and get me!" His voice rises with excitement as he tries to escape the slime, but he ignores all the vocabulary words and definitions on the screen.

10. Adventurer: One whose focus is on the discovery process
One student is collecting Internet facts to use in a research report. He scrolls up, looks at the picture of jellyfish, and says, "Oh,

wow!" He moves the mouse around the picture and taps it, and then he rolls the ball on the bottom of the mouse. Then he clicks back to http://izzy.online.discovery.com/area/nature/jellyfish/jellyfish2.html. Then he goes to *motion in the ocean* at http://izzy.online.discovery.com/area/nature/jellyfish/locomotion.html. "Oh, there's a nice cool jellyfish," he says.

11. Wanderer: One whose focus is on exploring without a destination

Two children sit at adjacent computers, working on different computer programs. One child clicks on the *Start* menu and scrolls up the list to try to find the software she was looking for. The second child asks, "What are you looking for?" She answers, "I don't know."

Technology Components

Varied Symbol Systems

Students in Ms. Coltrane's classroom made use of different aspects of technology as they used varied means of symbolic representation.

Elements of Exploration

Students explored the multiple symbol systems by navigating and manipulation.

Teacher's Instructional Goal

The teacher's instructional goal within the computer-based literacy event was defined by two areas: long term and short term. The short-term goal described the immediate purpose of the task at hand. The long-term goal described more far-reaching aspects of the task.

Mood or Key

The coding category Mood or Key describes the major affective elements that permeated the event.

Research and Data Summary

The Table includes a summary of the research questions and the data collection, preparation, and reduction and analysis.

Table
Summary of the Research Questions and the Data Collection, Preparation, and Reduction and Analysis

Questions	Data Collection	Data Preparation	Data Reduction and Analysis
1. What is the nature of the literacy curriculum in this classroom?	• field notes • informal and formal student and teacher interviews • samples of student work • transcripts of audiotaped interviews	• summarized field notes • transcribed relevant portions of administrator, teacher, and student interviews • selected key evidence to support analytic description of nature of literacy curriculum	• descriptive analysis to characterize literacy curriculum by Tone Kinds of Instruction Instructional Strategies Norms: a focus on process; the centrality of choice; a critical stance toward information resources; the use of class members as resources; risk-taking; a sense of caring and respect for others as members of a learning community
2. How do children participate in computer-based literacy events in this classroom within this instructional climate?	• field notes • informal and formal student and teacher interviews • samples of student work • transcriptions of audio interviews	• summarized field notes • transcribed relevant portions of student interviews • selected key evidence to support analysis of computer-based literacy event	• descriptive analysis • coding literacy events to categorize/capture the nature of the children's participation in computer-based literacy events by Themes Student Purpose (relational; task based) Roles Technology Components Instructional Goal Mood/Key

(continued)

Table (continued)
Summary of the Research Questions and the Data Collection, Preparation, and Reduction and Analysis

Questions	Data Collection	Data Preparation	Data Reduction and Analysis
3. How do children make use of different aspects of technology within computer-based literacy events as they a. use varied symbol systems in meaning construction, b. use cognitive explorations in meaning construction, and c. integrate affective elements in meaning construction?	• field notes • informal and formal student and teacher interviews • samples of student work • transcripts of audiotaped interviews	• summarized field notes • selected key evidence to support analysis of computer-based literacy event	• descriptive analysis • coding literacy events to categorize/capture the use of multiple symbol systems, cognitive explorations, and affective elements
4. What are the interrelations among these questions, and how does an understanding of them clarify the ways in which the use of technology can support and constrain early literacy development?	• field notes • informal and formal student and teacher interviews • samples of student work • transcripts of audiotaped interviews	• summarized vignettes • analyzed vignettes with regard to the research questions	• summary of research findings

Appendix B

Lesson Plans for Integrating Computer Use in the Classroom

Collaborative Internet Lesson

Tell your students that they are going to learn about amusement parks. Remind the students that, because there is so much information on this topic, you will need to work collaboratively to learn most effectively. The class should use the following amusement park physics website to begin their research: www.learner.org/exhibits/parkphysics.

1. Provide the class with a list of the following subtopics:
   Roller Coasters
   Carousel
   Bumper Cars
   Pendulum
   Free Fall
   As a class, decide how you will form small groups and how you will assign each group a topic.

2. Tell the students that each group is responsible for teaching the rest of the class about its assigned topic by giving a brief presentation. Each group should include new vocabulary, concepts, and a visual aid in its presentation.

3. After the groups are finished, provide the class with the Collaboration Rubric (see p. 119) to evaluate their collaborative efforts. Ask each student to rate the effectiveness of his or her group's effort by filling out the rubric.

Collaboration Rubric

Directions: Read each question and circle the number that matches your response.

1 = Definitely yes
2 = Somewhat
3 = Definitely no

	1	2	3
Was my group's collaboration a success?	1	2	3
Did each person feel comfortable asking for help?	1	2	3
Did one person know more than another person?	1	2	3
Did the group members help one another?	1	2	3

---

4. Lead a class discussion on what students learned from evaluating the success of their collaborations. Some questions you might want to use include the following:
   What did each student contribute to the collaboration?
   What did each student do to further the collaboration?
   What difficulties did the students encounter?
   What could the students do better next time?
5. Based on the discussion, create and post a class chart that highlights principles for effective collaborations.

Collaborative Role-Play Lesson

Read aloud the following scenarios to your students and ask them to role-play responses. They should role-play examples of what would happen in a good collaboration as well as what not to do. If possible, invite another class to view the exercise. After the students have role-played varied scenarios, invite feedback and critique the solutions offered.

Scenario 1: Imagine that you are working on the computer and it freezes. You ask your classmate sitting next to you for help. The person ignores you. What will you do?

Scenario 2: Imagine that you are using software that you also have at home. Your classmate sitting next to you is lost and becoming frustrated. What will you do?

Scenario 3: Imagine that you had an argument at recess with one of your classmates. When recess is over, your teacher assigns you to work together on an Internet research project. What will you do?

Internet Scavenger Hunt

The processes of collecting, analyzing, and planning gives structure to the students' research efforts. Try creating your own graphic organizer before conducting this activity with your students.

1. Show the students how to conduct an Internet search using the search engine at www.yahooligans.com. You will find helpful information on searching at the Yahooligans Teacher Guide at www.yahooligans.com/tg/search.html.

2. Divide the class into small groups and ask each group to collect five Internet facts on a topic that you are studying in class.

3. Post all the facts the students collected on a board and use the facts to create a graphic organizer. Note: Using a graphic organizer is considered more efficient than using an outline because the visual format shows relations between and among concepts (Robinson & Kiewra, 1995).

4. Read aloud each fact. Model how to create categories based on the collected facts. The Sample Graphic Organizer on p. 121 contains an example of an Internet-based graphic organizer.

5. Assign each group to conduct further research and create its own graphic organizer using one of the categories you have created in the class graphic organizer.

6. Ask each group to present the graphic organizer it has constructed to the entire class.

Top 10 Websites of the Month Lesson

Ask your students to create a list of websites that they have found enjoyable and interesting. You might assign one group of students to this task for a two- or four-week period. Then, host an end-of-the-month presen-

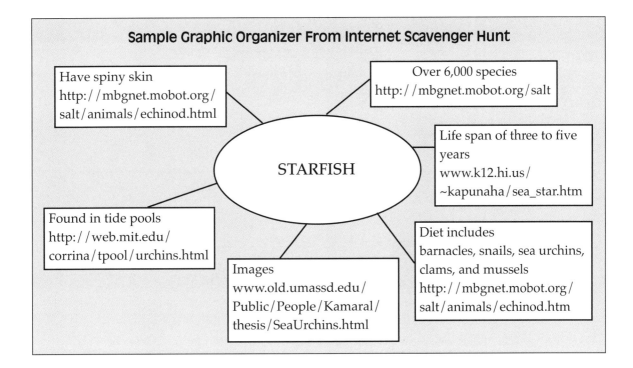

Sample Graphic Organizer From Internet Scavenger Hunt

tation during which students share their findings. You may wish to house your list on your own class webpage. Some resources for creating web-pages may be found at www.yahooligans.com/computers_games_and_online/world_wide_web/Web_Page_Design. If possible, invite other class-es in your school to participate by sharing their own favorite websites.

Enhancing Tales Lesson

Choose a familiar folk tale such as *The Three Little Bears* or *The Three Billy Goats Gruff*. Read aloud the tale to the class. Divide the students into small groups and ask each group to use the Internet as a resource to enhance the telling of the tale. Provide the students with the following lists of ideas and resources that they may use to enhance the tale selected.

Ideas

- Create a mural, poster, or playbill cover based on the tale by incor-porating photographs and images from the Internet.

- Add music files to enhance the tale.
- Make puppets to use in a performance of the tale.
- Create clay animation of the tale.
- Create a stage set for the tale.

Resources

Images:
- Google

  www.google.com (Click on *Images*, and type in what you are searching for.)

- Pics4Learning

  www.pics4learning.com/?search=cat&query=Animals_Goat
  www.pics4learning.com/index.php?search=qsearch&query=bridges

Music:
- ArtsAlive.Ca

  www.artsalive.ca/en/mus/musicresources/music.html

Puppets:
- UNICEF

  www.unicef.org/puppets

- Puppet Resource Center

  www.legendsandlore.com/puppet-resource.html

- American Animation at the Library of Congress site

  http://lcweb2.loc.gov/ammem/oahtml/oahome.html

- Clay-animated movie at Klick.org

  www.klick.org/kids/techietalk/animation/claymation

After the students have completed their enhancements, ask all the groups to share what they have done with the class. Discuss how a tale may be enriched by telling it in different ways.

Family Fun Night Lesson

Invite students and their families and friends to a Family Fun Night at your school. Have the students set up activities to highlight how they are using computers in the classroom. This may include demonstrations and hands-on opportunities for participation. You may wish to invite other classes to your event to share the fun.

References

Almasi, J.F. (1995). The nature of fourth graders' sociocognitive conflicts in peer-led and teacher-led discussions of literature. *Reading Research Quarterly, 30,* 314–351.

Alvermann, D.E., Moon, J.S., & Hagood, M.C. (1999). *Popular culture in the classroom: Teaching and researching critical media literacy.* Newark, DE: International Reading Association; Chicago: National Reading Conference.

Anderson-Inman, L., Horney, M.A., Chen, D., & Lewin, L. (1994). Hypertext literacy: Observations from the electrotext project. *Language Arts, 71*(4), 279–287.

The Amazing Writing Machine [Computer software]. (1996). Cambridge, MA: The Learning Company.

The American Girls Premiere [Computer software]. (1999). Cambridge, MA: The Learning Company.

Baker, E., & Kinzer, C.K. (1998). Effects of technology on process writing: Are they all good? In T. Shanahan & F.V. Rodriguez-Brown (Eds.), *47th yearbook of the National Reading Conference* (pp. 428–440). Chicago: National Reading Conference.

Bakhtin, M.M. (1986). *Speech genres and other late essays* (V.W. McGee, Trans.). Austin: University of Texas Press.

Berghoff, B. (1993). Moving towards aesthetic literacy in the first grade. In D.J. Leu & C.K. Kinzer (Eds.), *Examining central issues in literacy research, theory, and practice* (42nd yearbook of the National Reading Conference, pp. 217–226). Chicago: National Reading Conference.

Bikerts, S. (1995). *The Gutenberg elegies: The fate of reading in an electronic age.* New York: Ballantine.

Bogdan, R.C., & Biklen, S.K. (1992). *Qualitative research for education: An introduction to theory and methods.* Boston: Allyn & Bacon.

Bruffee, K.A. (1993). *Collaborative learning: Higher education, interdependence and the authority of knowledge.* Baltimore: Johns Hopkins University Press.

Bruner, J.S. (1985). On teaching thinking: An afterthought. In J.W. Segal, M. Chipman, & R. Glaser (Eds.), *Thinking and learning skills* (Vol. 1–2, pp. 597–608). Hillsdale, NJ: Erlbaum.

Cambourne, B. (2001). What do I do with the rest of the class? The nature of teaching–learning activities. *Language Arts, 79*(2), 124–135.

Cambourne, B., & Turbill, J. (1987). *Coping with chaos*. Portsmouth, NH: Heinemann.

Carroll, M. (1999). *Cartwheels on the keyboard: The role of technology in a first grade classroom*. Unpublished position paper, University of California at Berkeley.

Carroll, M. (2000). *Whitecaps on the keyboard: A voyage of discovery with computers in an elementary classroom*. Unpublished doctoral dissertation, University of California at Berkeley.

Cazden, C.B. (1976). Play with language and meta-linguistic awareness. In J.S. Bruner, A. Jolly, & K. Sylva (Eds.), *Play: Its role in development and evolution* (pp. 603–608). New York: Basic Books.

Cazden, C.B. (1988). *Classroom discourse: The language of teaching and learning*. Portsmouth, NH: Heinemann.

Chang, L.L., & Osguthorpe, R.T. (1990). The effects of computerized picture–word processing on kindergartners' language development. *Journal of Research in Childhood Education, 5*(1), 73–84.

Clay, M.M. (1975). *What did I write? Beginning writer behaviour.* Auckland, NZ: Heinemann.

Cohen, E.G. (1986). *Designing groupwork: Strategies for the heterogeneous classroom*. New York: Teachers College Press.

Cohen, E.G. (1994). Restructuring the classroom: Conditions for productive small groups. *Review of Educational Research, 64*(1), 1–35.

Csikszentmihalyi, M. (1990). Literacy and intrinsic motivation. *Daedalus, 119*(2), 115–140.

Daiute, C. (1988). The early development of writing abilities: Two theoretical perspectives. In J.L. Hoot & S.B. Silvern (Eds.), *Writing with computers in the early grades* (pp. 10–22). New York: Teachers College Press.

Daiute, C. (1989). Play as thought: Thinking strategies of young writers. *Harvard Educational Review, 59*, 1–23.

Dalton, B., & Grisham, D.L. (2002, March). Taking a position on integrating literacy and technology in the curriculum. *Reading Online, 5*(7). Retrieved March 24, 2002, from http://www.readingonline.org/editorial/edit_index.asp?HREF=/editorial/march2002/index.html

Dyson, A.H. (1989). *Multiple worlds of child writers: Friends learning to write*. New York: Teachers College Press.

Dyson, A.H. (1991). Viewpoints: The word and the world—Reconceptualizing written language development or do rainbows mean a lot to little girls? *Research in the Teaching of English, 25*(1), 97–123.

Dyson, A.H. (1993). *Social worlds of children learning to write in an urban primary school*. New York: Teachers College Press.

Eisner, E.W. (1978). The impoverished mind. *Educational Leadership, 35*(8), 615–623.

Fish, S. (1980). *Is there a text in this class? The authority of interpretive communities*. Cambridge, MA: Harvard University Press.

Franklin, M.B. (1983). Play as the creation of imaginary situations. In S. Wapner & B. Kaplan (Eds.), *Toward a holistic developmental psychology* (pp. 197–220). Hillsdale, NJ: Erlbaum.

Freedman, S.W. (1994). *Exchanging writing, exchanging cultures: Lessons in school reform from the United States and Great Britain*. Cambridge, MA: Harvard University Press.

Gambrell, L.B. (1996). Creating classroom cultures that foster reading motivation. *The Reading Teacher, 50*, 14–25.

Geertz, C. (1973). *The interpretation of cultures: Selected essays*. New York: Basic Books.

Grisham, D.L. (2001, February). Making technology meaningful for literacy teaching: A webquest. *Reading Online, 4*(7). Retrieved August 18, 2002, from http://www.readingonline.org/editorial/edit_index.asp?HREF=/editorial/february2001/index.html

Gundlach, R., McLane, J.B., Stott, F.M., & McNamee, G.D. (1985). The social foundations of children's early writing development. In M. Farr (Ed.), *Advances in writing: Vol. 1. Children's early writing development* (pp. 1–58). Norwood, NJ: Ablex.

Harste, J.C. (1994). Literacy as curricular conversations about knowledge, inquiry and morality. In R.B. Ruddell, M.R. Ruddell, & H. Singer (Eds.), *Theoretical models and processes of reading* (4th ed., pp. 1220–1242). Newark, DE: International Reading Association.

Harste, J.C., Burke, C.L., & Woodward, V.A. (1994). Children's language and world: Initial encounters with print. In R.B. Ruddell, M.R. Ruddell, & H. Singer (Eds.), *Theoretical models and processes of reading* (4th ed., pp. 48–69). Newark, DE: International Reading Association.

Hartup, W.W. (1996). The company they keep: Friendships and their developmental significance. *Child Development, 67*(1), 1–13.

Hillinger, M.L. (1992). Computer speech and responsive text: Hypermedia support for reading instruction. *Reading and Writing: An Interdisciplinary Journal, 4*(2), 219–229.

International Reading Association. (2002). *Integrating literacy and technology in the curriculum. A position statement of the International Reading Association*. Retrieved July 3, 2002, from http://www.reading.org/positions/technology.html

Johnson, D.W., & Johnson, R.T. (1987). *Learning together and alone: Cooperative, competitive, and individualistic learning* (2nd ed.). Englewood Cliffs, NJ: Prentice Hall.

Kagan, S. (1990). A structural approach to cooperative learning. *Educational Leadership, 47*(4), 12–15.

Kamil, M., & Lane, D. (1998). Researching the relation between technology and literacy: An agenda for the 21st century. In D. Reinking, M.C. McKenna, L.D. Labbo, & R.D. Kieffer (Eds.), *Handbook of literacy and technology: Transformations in a post-typographic world* (pp. 323–341). Mahwah, NJ: Erlbaum.

Kinzer, C., & Leu, D.J., Jr. (1997). The challenge of change: Exploring literacy and learning in electronic environments. *Language Arts, 74*(2), 126–136.

Labbo, L.D. (1996). A semiotic analysis of young children's symbol making in a classroom computer center. *Reading Research Quarterly, 31*, 356–385.

Labbo, L.D., & Kuhn, M. (1998). Electronic symbol making: Young children's computer-related emerging concepts about literacy. In D. Reinking, M.C. McKenna, L.D. Labbo, & R.D. Kieffer (Eds.), *Handbook of literacy and technology: Transformations in a post-typographic world* (pp. 79–91). Mahwah, NJ: Erlbaum.

Langer, J. (1987). A sociocognitive perspective on literacy. In J. Langer (Ed.), *Language, literacy and culture: Issues in society and school* (pp. 1–20). Norwood, NJ: Ablex.

Leu, D.J., Jr. (1996). Sarah's secret: Social aspects of literacy and learning in a digital information age. *The Reading Teacher, 50*, 162–165.

Leu, D.J., Jr. (1997). Caity's question: Literacy as deixis on the Internet. *The Reading Teacher, 51*, 62–67.

Leu, D.J., Jr. (2000). Our children's future: Changing the focus of literacy and literacy instruction. *The Reading Teacher, 53*, 424–429.

Leu, D.J., Jr. (2002). The new literacies: Research on reading instruction with the Internet. In A.E. Farstrup & S.J. Samuels (Eds.), *What research has to say about reading instruction* (3rd ed., pp. 310–336). Newark, DE: International Reading Association.

Leu, D.J., Jr., & Kinzer, C.K. (2000). The convergence of literacy instruction with networked technologies for information and communication. *Reading Research Quarterly, 35*, 108–127.

Leu, D.J., Jr., & Leu, D.D. (1999). *Teaching with the Internet: Lessons from the classroom.* Norwood, MA: Christopher-Gordon.

Leu, D.J., Jr., Mallette, M.H., & Karchmer, R.A. (2001). New literacies, new technologies, and new realities: Toward an agenda for the literacy research community. *Reading Research and Instruction: Themed Issue on Literacy and Technology, 40*, 265–272.

Leu, D.J., Jr., & Reinking, D.P. (1996). Bringing insights from reading research to research on electronic learning environments. In H. van Oostendorp & S. de Mul (Eds.), *Cognitive aspects of electronic text processing* (pp. 43–76). Norwood, NJ: Ablex.

Luke, C. (2000). Cyber-schooling and technological change: Multiliteracies for new times. In B. Cope & M. Kalantzis (Eds.), *Multiliteracies: Literacy learning and the design of social futures* (pp. 69–91). London: Routledge.

Magic School Bus Explores the Ocean [Computer software]. (1996). New York: Scholastic.

Mallette, M.H., Karchmer, R.A., & Leu, D.J., Jr. (2001). An invitation: Exploring the new literacies of our future. *Reading Research and Instruction, 40*(3), 157–158.

Math Blaster [Computer software]. (1997). Torrance, CA: Davidson.

Mathewson, G.C. (1994). Model of attitude influence upon reading and learning to read. In R.B. Ruddell, M.R. Ruddell, & H. Singer (Eds.), *Theoretical models and processes of reading* (4th ed., pp. 1131–1161). Newark, DE: International Reading Association.

Mehan, H. (1982). The structure of classroom events and their consequences for student performance. In P. Gilmore & A.A. Glatthorn (Eds.), *Children in and out of school: Ethnography and education* (pp. 59–87). Washington, DC: Center for Applied Linguistics.

Metsala, J. (1996). Children's motivations in reading. *The Reading Teacher, 50,* 360–362.

Molinelli, P. (2000). *"Kind of like jazz": Reader stance, shared authority, and identity in a twelfth-grade English course.* Unpublished doctoral dissertation, University of California at Berkeley.

Moll, L.C. (1994). Literacy research in community and classrooms: A sociocultural approach. In R.B. Ruddell, M.R. Ruddell, & H. Singer (Eds.), *Theoretical models and processes of reading* (4th ed., pp. 179–207). Newark, DE: International Reading Association.

Pianfetti, E.S. (2001). Teachers and technology: Digital literacy through professional development. *Language Arts, 78*(3), 255–262.

Raphael, T.E., & McMahon, S.I. (1994). Book Club: An alternative framework for reading instruction. *The Reading Teacher, 48,* 102–116.

Reading Blaster [Computer software]. (1997). Torrance, CA: Davidson.

Reinking, D. (1997). *Me and my hypertext: A multiple digression analysis of technology and literacy (sic).* Retrieved December 17, 1998, from http://www.readingonline.org/articles/art_index.asp?HREF=hypertext/index.html

Reinking, D., McKenna, M.C., Labbo, L.D., & Kieffer, R.D. (Eds.). (1998). *Handbook of literacy and technology: Transformations in a post-typographic world.* Mahwah, NJ: Erlbaum.

Robinson, D.H, & Kiewra, K.A. (1995). Visual argument: Graphic organizers are superior to outlines in improving learning from text. *Journal of Educational Psychology, 87*(3), 455–467.

Rose, D.H., & Meyer, A. (1994). The role of technology in language arts instruction. *Language Arts, 71*(4), 290–294.

Ruddell, R.B. (1994). The development of children's comprehension and motivation during storybook discussion. In R.B. Ruddell, M.R. Ruddell, & H. Singer (Eds.), *Theoretical models and processes of reading* (4th ed., pp. 281–296). Newark, DE: International Reading Association.

Ruddell, R.B. (1999). *Teaching children to read and write: Becoming an influential teacher.* Boston: Allyn & Bacon.

Ruddell, R.B., & Unrau, N.J. (1994). Reading as a meaning-construction process: The reader, the text, and the teacher. In R.B. Ruddell, M.R. Ruddell, & H. Singer (Eds.), *Theoretical models and processes of reading* (4th ed., pp. 996–1056). Newark, DE: International Reading Association.

Salomon, G. (1979). *Interaction of media, cognition, and learning.* San Francisco: Jossey-Bass.

Schmar-Dobler, E. (2003). Reading on the Internet: The link between literacy and technology. *Journal of Adolescent & Adult Literacy*, *47*(1). Retrieved July 17, 2003, from http://www.readingonline.org/newliteracies/lit_index.asp? HREF=/newliteracies/jaal9-03_column/index.html

Short, K.G., Kaufman, G., & Kahn, L.H. (2000). "I just need to draw": Responding to literature across multiple sign systems. *The Reading Teacher*, *54*, 160–171.

Shulman, L.S., & Carey, N.B. (1984). Psychology and the limitations of individual rationality: Implications for the study of reasoning and civility. *Review of Educational Research*, *54*(4), 501–524.

Silva, C., & Delgado-Larocco, E.L. (1993). Facilitating learning through interconnections: A concept approach to core literature units. *Language Arts*, *70*(6), 469–474.

Slavin, R.E. (1983). *Cooperative learning*. New York: Longman.

Stoll, C. (1995). *Silicon snake oil: Second thoughts on the information highway*. New York: Doubleday.

Sutherland-Smith, W. (2002). Weaving the literacy web: Changes in reading from page to screen. *The Reading Teacher*, *55*, 662–669.

Tizard, B., & Hughes, M. (1984). *Young children learning*. Cambridge, MA: Harvard University Press.

Vygotsky, L.S. (1978). *Mind in society: The development of higher psychological processes* (M. Cole, V. John-Steiner, S. Scribner, & E. Souberman. Eds. & Trans.). Cambridge, MA: Harvard University Press. (Original work published 1934)

Vygotsky, L.S. (1986). *Thought and language* (A. Kozalin, Trans.). Cambridge, MA: MIT Press. (Original work published 1934)

Index

Note: Page references followed by *b* or *f* indicate boxes or figures, respectively.

CARROLL, M., 14, 72, 87

CAZDEN, C.B., 22, 22*b*, 87

CHANG, L.L., 87

CHEN, D., 71, 103

CHOICE: centrality of, 44–45; and computer use, 51; and exploration, 68–71; Reflection Points on, 45

CLASSROOM: introducing computer technology to, 1–16; literacy activities in, 19–22; norms of, 39; role of computers in, 32–35; as setting, 7–10

CLASSROOM COMMUNITY, 37–38; implementation of, 50–53; Reflection Points on, 37–38, 53–54; voices and values in, 36–54

COHEN, E.G., 56

COLLABORATION, 13, 55–66; versus collision, 60–62; equitable, 57–60; implementation of, 65–66; lesson plan for, 118–120; mutual delight in, 63–65; Reflection Points on, 57, 59–60, 66; research on, 109; rubric on, 119*f*

COLLISIONS: Reflection Points on, 62

COMMUNITY. *See* classroom community

COMPUTER TECHNOLOGY: appropriate use of, 94–97; choice and, 51; collaboration and, 55–66; definition of, 5; exploration and, 67–83; findings on, 13–15; future of, 102–105; introduction to classroom, 1–16; and language, 29–32; and literacy development, 24–26; play with, 13, 84–100; Reflection Points on, 3–4, 31, 35; resources on, 4*b*; role in classroom, 32–35; and symbol systems used, 26–29

COMPUTER TECHNOLOGY INTEGRATION: challenges and opportunities in, 101–108; future of, 102–105; implementation of, 106–107; Reflection Points on, 105–107; strategies for, 104*f*

CRITICAL STANCE: toward information sources, 45–46, 51

CSIKSZENTMIHALYI, M., 75

CURRICULUM, LITERACY, 38–39; integrating technology into, 104*f*

D

DAIUTE, C., 30, 99

DALTON, B., 102

DELGADO-LAROCCO, E.L., 99

DIALOGUE: Reflection Points on, 23; resources on, 22*b*; small-group, 23–24; whole-class, 19–22

DRAFTING, 40*f*

DYSON, A.H., 22, 27, 29, 31, 65, 82, 100